Spelling for Literacy

FOR AGES 8-9

Andrew Brodie

This second edition published 2015 by
Bloomsbury Publishing Plc

50 Bedford Square
London
WC1B 3DP
UK

1385 Broadway
New York
NY 10018
USA

www.bloomsbury.com

Bloomsbury is a registered trademark of Bloomsbury Publishing Plc

First published 2001 by Andrew Brodie Publications

British Library Cataloguing-in-Publication Data
A catalogue record for this book is available from the British Library.

ISBN 978-1-4729-1657-0

Library of Congress Cataloging-in-Publication Data
A catalog record for this book is available from the Library of Congress.

1 3 5 7 9 10 8 6 4 2

Printed and bound in India by Replika Press Pvt. Ltd

This book is produced using paper that is made from wood grown in managed, sustainable forests. It is natural, renewable and recyclable. The logging and manufacturing processes conform to the environmental regulations of the country of origin.

To view more of our titles please visit www.bloomsbury.com

B L O O M S B U R Y

Contents

Set 1	Unusual tense changes	6
Set 2	Changing **f** to **v** when creating plurals	9
Set 3	Endings **tion** and **ious**	12
Set 4	Prefix **al**	15
Set 5	Words beginning **ad**	18
Set 6	Words beginning **att**, **ass** and **aff**	21
Set 7	Mixed words	24
Set 8	**it's**, **its**, and the ending **ive**	27
Set 9	**ou** and **au**	30
Set 10	Double **s**	33
Set 11	Suffixes **ness** and **ment**	36
Set 12	Homophones and near homophones	39
Set 13	Suffixes **en** and **ate**	42
Set 14	Suffixes **ise** and **fy**	45
Set 15	Compound words	48
Set 16	Suffix **ly**	51
Set 17	Endings **ible** and **ible**	54
Set 18	Sound **i** spelt **y**	57
Set 19	Prefixes **in** and **il**	60
Set 20	Prefixes **ir** and **anti**	63
Set 21	Prefixes **inter** and **sub**	66
Set 22	**graph**, **auto** and **im**	69
Set 23	Adding suffixes, and words beginning **inter**	72
Set 24	Endings **ly** and **ally**	75
Set 25	Creating words from others	78
Set 26	Ending **sion** with **j** sound spelt **s**; words with **v**	81
Set 27	Endings **our** and **us**	84
Set 28	Endings **sion**, **sive** and **tion**	87
Set 29	Endings **cian** and **al**	90
Set 30	Micro and mini	93
Set 31	Hard **ch**, soft **sc**	96
Set 32	Apostrophes to show possession	99
Set 33	Word list for Years 3 and 4	102
Set 34	Word list for Years 3 and 4	105
Set 35	Word list for Years 3 and 4	108
Set 36	Word list for Years 3 and 4	111
Set 37	Word list for Years 3 and 4	114
Set 38	Word list for Years 3 and 4	117
Set 39	Word list for Years 3 and 4	120
Set 40	Unusual suffixes	123

Introduction

The Spelling for Literacy series is well established as the leading spelling resource in use in schools across the United Kingdom. Now fully updated to meet the demands of the new National Curriculum, teachers can feel confident that each book covers all the spellings required for their year group.

This is the fourth book in the series, covering spellings suitable for Year 4 arising from the sounds, suffixes and prefixes that are specified as statutory requirements for Years 3 and 4.
All the non-statutory example words listed in the National Curriculum are also included, together with other words that follow similar patterns.

As stated in the National Curriculum, Year 3 and Year 4 pupils should be reminded of the rules for adding suffixes that they have met in Key Stage 1.

In this book they learn the use of more suffixes as well as a range of prefixes. They also learn about homophones and near homophones.In a working environment of praise and enjoyment, the activities contained in this book will provide ample opportunities for meeting the statutory requirements as shown below.

Work for Year 3 and 4

STATUTORY REQUIREMENTS

- Adding suffixes beginning with vowel letters to words of more than one syllable
- The /ɪ/ sound spelt y elsewhere than at the end of words
- The /ʌ/ sound spelt ou
- More prefixes
- The suffix –ation
- The suffix –ly
- Words with endings sounding like /ʒə/ or /tʃə/
- Endings which sound like /ʒən/
- The suffix –ous
- Endings which sound like /ʃən/, spelt –tion, –sion, –ssion, –cian
- Words with the /k/ sound spelt ch (Greek in origin)
- Words with the /ʃ/ sound spelt ch (mostly French in origin)
- Words ending with the /g/ sound spelt – gue and the /k/ sound spelt –que (French in origin)
- Words with the /s/ sound spelt sc (Latin in origin)
- Words with the /eɪ/ sound spelt ei, eigh, or ey
- Possessive apostrophe with plural words
- Homophones and near-homophones

Suggestions for using this book...

The words are arranged in sets, usually of ten words but in some cases twelve or sixteen. Each set of words is used in three styles of sheet:

Overview
UNUSUAL TENSE CHANGES

SET 1 SHEET A

shoot	shot
catch	caught
fight	fought
hear	heard
shake	shook
wear	wore
creep	crept
break	broke

SHEET A

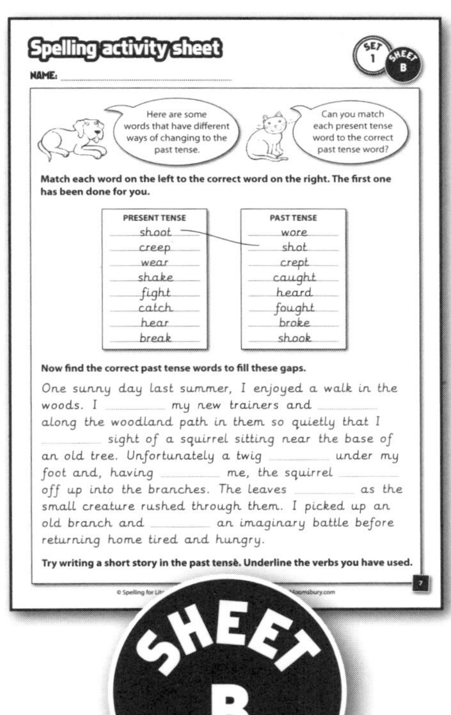

Spelling activity sheet

SET 1 SHEET B

NAME: ....

Match each word on the left to the correct word on the right. The first one has been done for you.

PRESENT TENSE	PAST TENSE
shoot	wore
creep	shot
wear	crept
shake	caught
fight	heard
catch	fought
hear	broke
break	shook

Now find the correct past tense words to fill these gaps.

One sunny day last summer, I enjoyed a walk in the woods. I ________ my new trainers and ________ along the woodland path in them so quietly that I ________ sight of a squirrel sitting near the base of an old tree. Unfortunately a twig ________ under my foot and, having ________ me, the squirrel ________ off up into the branches. The leaves ________ as the small creature rushed through them. I picked up an old branch and ________ an imaginary battle before returning home tired and hungry.

Try writing a short story in the past tense. Underline the verbs you have used.

SHEET B

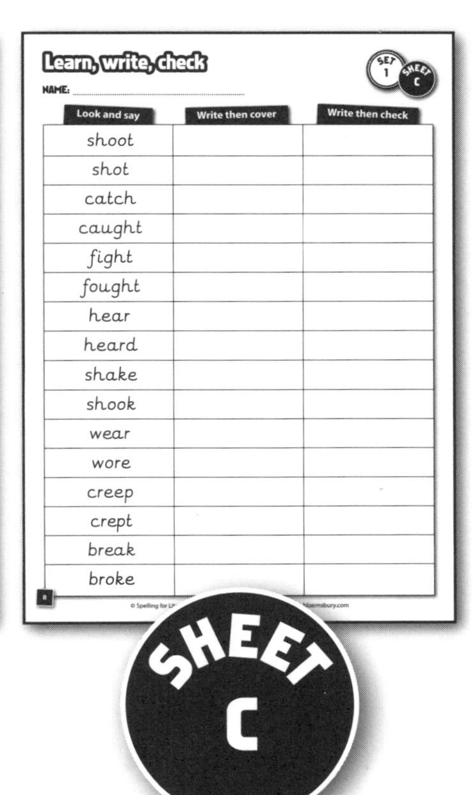

Learn, write, check

SET 1 SHEET C

NAME: ....

Look and say	Write then cover	Write then check
shoot		
shot		
catch		
caught		
fight		
fought		
hear		
heard		
shake		
shook		
wear		
wore		
creep		
crept		
break		
broke		

SHEET C

Overview

- Can be displayed on-screen for discussion.
- Can be printed out and displayed as 'Words of the Week'.

Spelling activity sheet

- To be used as part of a lesson.
- A perfect follow-up activity for the learning that has taken place using Sheet A and ideal for homework.

Learn, write, check

- Children look at the words, say them out loud and write them down, before covering the first two columns, re-writing the words and then checking them.
- Can be used in class.
- Can be used as homework.

Overview

UNUSUAL TENSE CHANGES

shoot	shot
catch	caught
fight	fought
hear	heard
shake	shook
wear	wore
creep	crept
break	broke

NAME: ______________________________

Here are some words that have different ways of changing to the past tense.

Can you match each present tense word to the correct past tense word?

Match each word on the left to the correct word on the right. The first one has been done for you.

PRESENT TENSE	PAST TENSE
shoot	wore
creep	shot
wear	crept
shake	caught
fight	heard
catch	fought
hear	broke
break	shook

Now find the correct past tense words to fill these gaps.

One sunny day last summer, I enjoyed a walk in the woods. I __________ my new trainers and __________ along the woodland path in them so quietly that I __________ sight of a squirrel sitting near the base of an old tree. Unfortunately a twig __________ under my foot and, having __________ me, the squirrel __________ off up into the branches. The leaves __________ as the small creature rushed through them. I picked up an old branch and __________ an imaginary battle before returning home tired and hungry.

Try writing a short story in the past tense. Underline the verbs you have used.

Learn, write, check

NAME: ______________________

Look and say	Write then cover	Write then check
shoot		
shot		
catch		
caught		
fight		
fought		
hear		
heard		
shake		
shook		
wear		
wore		
creep		
crept		
break		
broke		

Overview

CHANGING F TO V WHEN CREATING PLURALS

calf	calves
half	halves
self	selves
cliff	cliffs
sniff	sniffs
knife	knives
life	lives
safe	saves

Spelling activity sheet

NAME: ______________________________

Many singular words just have **s** added to make them plural.

Words ending with a single **f** or **fe** usually change to **ves** to become plurals.

The answers to the clues below are all plural words. The singular version of each answer is in the box below, to help you.

glove	leaf	calf	half	wolf	knife

These grow into cows. ______________

These are two equal pieces. ______________

These grow on trees. ______________

Use these to cut things. ______________

These are wild animals, like dogs. ______________

You wear these on your hands. ______________

Now make up some clues of your own for the following words.

loaves ______________________________

scarves ______________________________

elves ______________________________

Try to write down ten words ending in 'ff'. What happens when you make these words into plurals? With a friend, discuss what you have discovered.

Learn, write, check

NAME: ____________________

Look and say	Write then cover	Write then check
calf		
calves		
half		
halves		
self		
selves		
cliff		
cliffs		
sniff		
sniffs		
knife		
knives		
life		
lives		
safe		
saves		

Overview

ENDINGS TION AND IOUS

station	ration
competition	question
action	reaction
information	subtraction
serious	ferocious
obvious	previous
curious	glorious
delicious	suspicious

Spelling activity sheet

NAME: ______________________________

Many words end in **tion**…

…and many more end in **ious.**

Find the 'tion' and 'ious' words in the word bank below. Write them in the correct word safes and cross them out when you have found them.

WORD SAFE: tion	**WORD SAFE: ious**

Now, reading each line from left to right, write down the useful information from the words that are left.

Learn, write, check

NAME: ______________________

Look and say	Write then cover	Write then check
station		
ration		
competition		
question		
action		
reaction		
information		
subtraction		
serious		
ferocious		
obvious		
previous		
curious		
glorious		
delicious		
suspicious		

ways	always
arm	alarm
so	also
most	almost
one	alone
ready	already
together	altogether
though	although

Spelling activity sheet

NAME: ______________________________

This page is about the prefix **al**.

al sometimes means 'the' or 'all'.

Follow the clues to fill in the word triangle.
Use the words in the box to help you.

almost although also altogether alone already

1. As well
2. By myself
3. Nearly
4. By this time
5. Even though
6. Totally

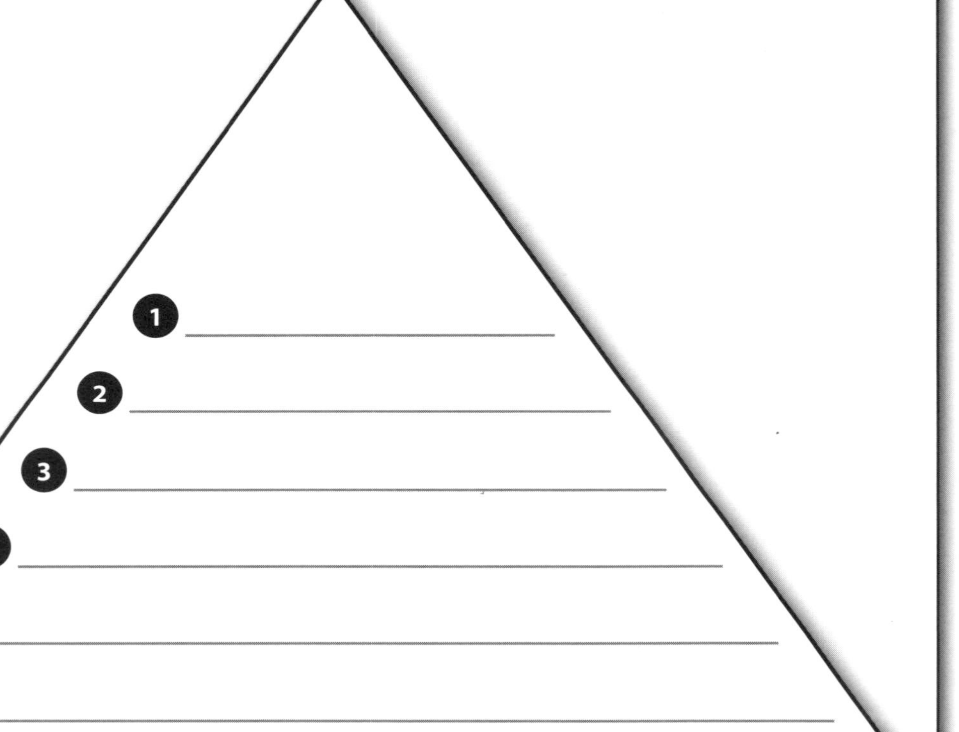

Write a definition for each of the following words. Use a dictionary to help you.

alarm ______________________________

always ______________________________

allure ______________________________

allot ______________________________

(Please note: **allot** is not the same thing as **a lot**.)

Learn, write, check

NAME: ____________________

Look and say	Write then cover	Write then check
ways		
always		
arm		
alarm		
so		
also		
most		
almost		
one		
alone		
ready		
already		
together		
altogether		
though		
although		

verb	adverb
apt	adapt
venture	adventure
join	adjoin
admit	adjust
advert	addition
admire	adopt
address	advance

Spelling activity sheet

NAME: 

The prefix **ad** sometimes alters words.

The prefix **ad** in front of a word usually means 'going towards'.

Follow the clues to fill in the word triangle. Use the words in the box to help you.

adopt	adapt	address	adjust	admire
advance	adverb	adventure	addition	

1. Take into a new family
2. Regard with pleasure
3. Go towards
4. Totalling numbers
5. A daring activity
6. To put in the correct position
7. Put this on an envelope
8. A word that sometimes accompanies a verb
9. To change something

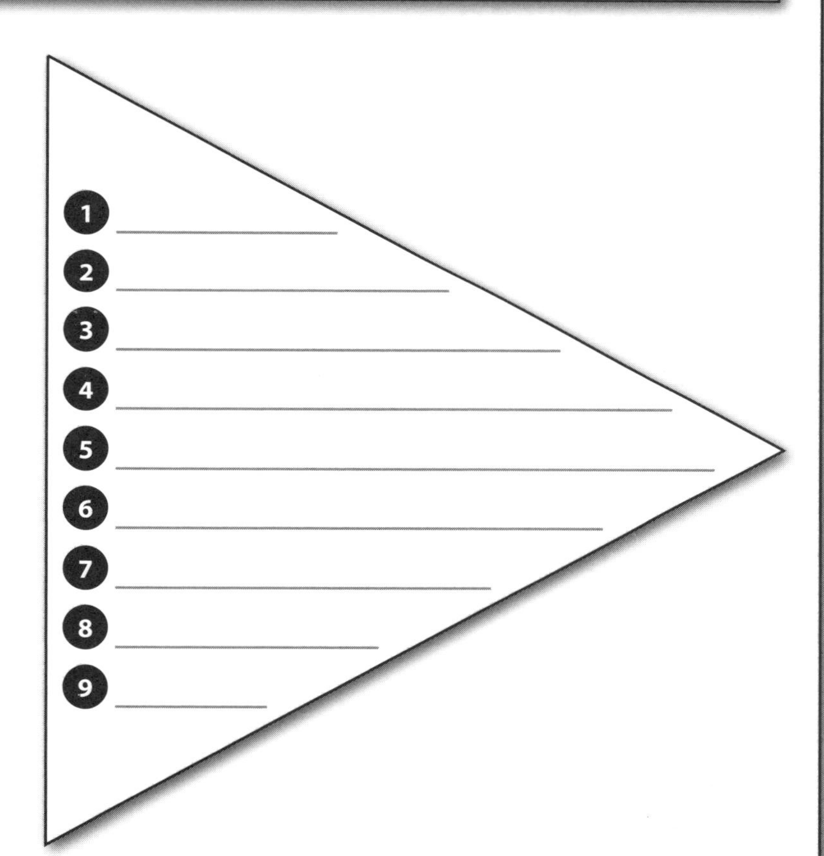

Write a definition for each of the following words. Use a dictionary to help you.

admit ______________________________

adjust ______________________________

adjoin ______________________________

advert ______________________________

Learn, write, check

NAME:

Look and say	Write then cover	Write then check
verb		
adverb		
apt		
adapt		
venture		
adventure		
join		
adjoin		
admit		
adjust		
advert		
addition		
admire		
adopt		
address		
advance		

WORDS BEGINNING ATT, ASS AND AFF

assemble	assembly
assist	assistant
assort	assortment
attract	attractive
attend	attendance
affix	affirm
afflict	affliction
affection	affectionate

Spelling activity sheet

NAME: ______________________________

When you have school assembly…

…everybody assembles in the hall.

Try to fit the correct words into the sentences.

attend	assortment	affectionate
assemble	attractive	

1. There is a very good ______________ of chocolates in the box.
2. My dog is a very ______________ pet.
3. I ______________ school every day.
4. The flowers in the garden were very ______________.
5. When the fire alarm sounds we all ______________ in the playground.

Write a definition for each of the following words. Use a dictionary to help you.

affirm ______________________________

attend ______________________________

affix ______________________________

affliction ______________________________

Learn, write, check

NAME: ______________________

Look and say	Write then cover	Write then check
assemble		
assembly		
assist		
assistant		
assort		
assortment		
attract		
attractive		
attend		
attendance		
affix		
affirm		
afflict		
affliction		
affection		
affectionate		

MIXED WORDS

bright	flight
alone	aloft
attract	admire
again	ascend
avenue	special
station	enough
subtraction	correction
through	suspicious

Spelling activity sheet

NAME: ____________________

Word beginnings are called **prefixes**…

…and word endings are **suffixes**.

Sort these words and post them in the correct boxes.

correction	subtraction	alone	attract
aloft	suspicious	bright	again
through	flight	enough	special
ascend	avenue	station	admire

af at as al	ad a	ight ough	ial tion ious

Find four more words that could go in each box.

Learn, write, check

NAME: ______________________

Look and say	Write then cover	Write then check
bright		
flight		
alone		
aloft		
attract		
admire		
again		
ascend		
avenue		
special		
station		
enough		
subtraction		
correction		
through		
suspicious		

Overview

IT'S, ITS AND THE ENDING IVE

it's	its
active	captive
forgive	motive
native	massive
expensive	relative
competitive	inquisitive
expansive	corrosive
decisive	attractive

Spelling activity sheet

SET 8 SHEET B

NAME: ______________________________

Use **its** without an apostrophe to mean **belonging to**.

Put 'it's' or 'its' correctly in the following sentences.

1. The skipping rope had lost ______ handle.
2. I think ______ wonderful having a holiday.
3. ______ getting late so I should go home now.
4. The cat will defend ______ territory.
5. ______ a bright sunny day.

Now complete each of these sentences with a word ending in 'ive'.
The words you will need are in the box.

active	competitive	massive
captive	relative	expensive

6. Gold jewellery is very ______________.
7. A gymnast is very ______________.
8. A prisoner is a ______________.
9. Something very large is ______________.
10. My uncle is a ______________.
11. I like to win as I am very ______________.

Learn, write, check

NAME:

Look and say	Write then cover	Write then check
it's		
its		
active		
captive		
forgive		
motive		
native		
massive		
expensive		
relative		
competitive		
inquisitive		
expansive		
corrosive		
decisive		
attractive		

trouble	found
around	journey
route	pour
four	young
taught	caught
aunt	autumn
haunt	cause
because	sausage

Spelling activity sheet

NAME: 

The vowel digraph **ou** can sound like **or**, **ow**, **oo** or **ur**. Try reading the words in the box that have **ou** in them.

Now look at the words that have got **au** in them. Does the **au** always sound the same?

ground	trousers	aunt
sausage	poured	because
through	journey	favourite
thought	autumn	route

Read the passage with care. Fill in the spaces using the correct words from the box above.

One warm __________ day my __________ decided to go for a walk. She took her __________ __________ past the football __________ and __________ the park. As she passed a cafe she __________ she felt peckish so she ordered a cup of tea and a __________ roll. The waiter tripped! The hot tea __________ all over my aunt and the teapot fell to the __________ with a clatter. Her __________ home was very hasty __________ she needed to put on a dry jumper and some dry __________!

Write ten more 'au' words and ten more 'ou' words. Include as many of them as you can in just four sentences. Read your sentences to a friend.

Learn, write, check

NAME: ______________________

Look and say	Write then cover	Write then check
trouble		
found		
around		
journey		
route		
pour		
four		
young		
taught		
caught		
aunt		
autumn		
haunt		
cause		
because		
sausage		

mission	impossible
missile	hassle
passion	passive
lesson	session
pass	fuss
process	guess
kiss	impress
boss	hiss

Spelling activity sheet

NAME: ______________________

Many words have **ss** at the end or in the middle.

You will not find words beginning with **ss**.

Follow the clues to answer these word puzzles. The answers are all 'ss' words. Use the words in the box to help you. Take care; there are more words in the box than you need!

passion	impress	passive	lessen	hiss
lesson	missile	impossible	mission	kiss
missing	guess	passing		

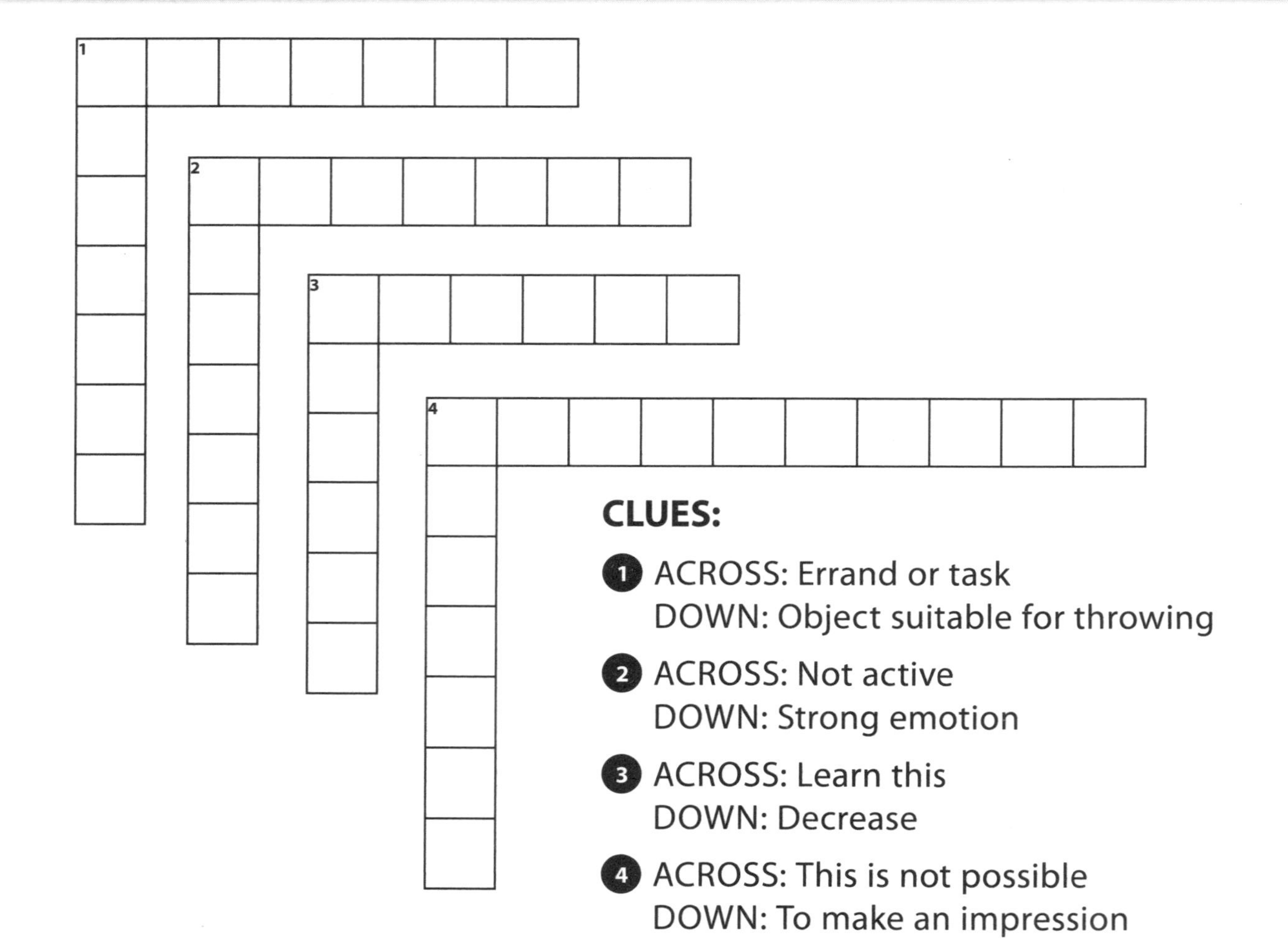

CLUES:

1. ACROSS: Errand or task
   DOWN: Object suitable for throwing
2. ACROSS: Not active
   DOWN: Strong emotion
3. ACROSS: Learn this
   DOWN: Decrease
4. ACROSS: This is not possible
   DOWN: To make an impression

Work with a partner. For each letter of the alphabet, try to find a word with 'ss' in. Are there any letters that you cannot find an 'ss' word for?

Learn, write, check

NAME: ______________________

Look and say	Write then cover	Write then check
mission		
impossible		
missile		
hassle		
passion		
passive		
lesson		
session		
pass		
fuss		
process		
guess		
kiss		
impress		
boss		
hiss		

Overview

SUFFIXES NESS AND MENT

sadness	kindness
silliness	happiness
drowsiness	darkness
softness	hardness
agreement	appointment
merriment	enjoyment
entertainment	engagement
government	endearment

NAME: ______________________________

When a word ends with a **y**, change **y** to **i** before adding **ness** or **ment**…

Unless the **y** follows a vowel, in which case it stays as **y**.

Look:

happy ⟶ happiness

employ ⟶ employment

Add 'ment'or 'ness' to each of these words to make new words.

merry	→ ________	silly	→ ________
sad	→ ________	drowsy	→ ________
dark	→ ________	endear	→ ________
engage	→ ________	soft	→ ________
hard	→ ________	happy	→ ________
kind	→ ________	agree	→ ________
entertain	→ ________	appoint	→ ________
govern	→ ________	enjoy	→ ________

Use a dictionary to help you to write a definition for each of the following words.

endearment ______________________________

government ______________________________

appointment ______________________________

Learn, write, check

NAME: ______________________

Look and say	Write then cover	Write then check
sadness		
kindness		
silliness		
happiness		
drowsiness		
darkness		
softness		
hardness		
agreement		
appointment		
merriment		
enjoyment		
entertainment		
engagement		
government		
endearment		

Overview

HOMOPHONES AND NEAR HOMOPHONES

to	too
two	there
their	they're
night	knight
pair	pear
eight	ate
stare	stair
see	sea

Spelling activity sheet

NAME: ______________________________

Some words can sound the same but are spelt differently and mean different things.

These words are called homophones.

Here are some examples of homophones:

1. *to (I am going to...)*
2. *two (the number)*
3. *too (also)*

Illustrate the following words in the boxes below.

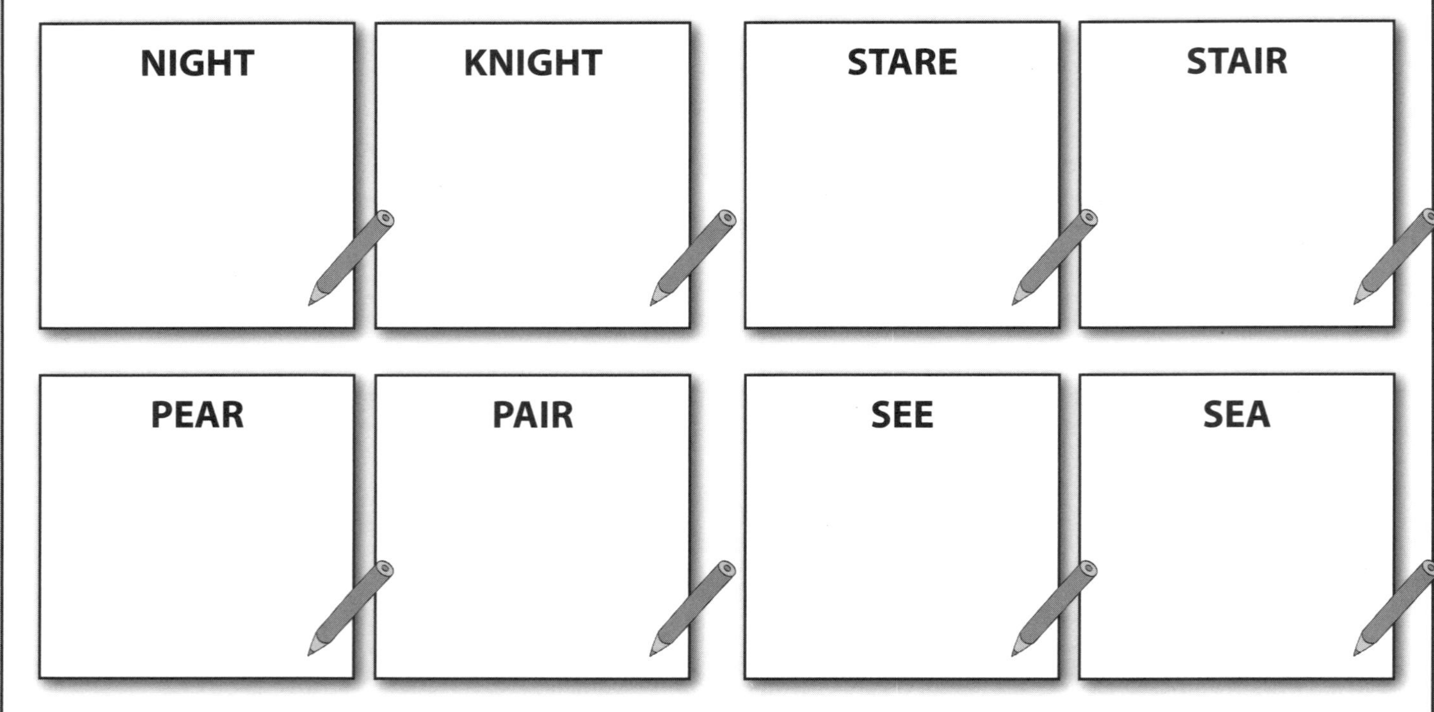

Use the following words in three sentences and write them on a separate piece of paper.

1. *there (a place)*
2. *their (belonging to)*
3. *they're (they are)*

Try to find more pairs of words that sound the same but are spelt differently. Can you illustrate them?

Learn, write, check

NAME: ______________________________

Look and say	Write then cover	Write then check
to		
too		
two		
there		
their		
they're		
night		
knight		
pair		
pear		
eight		
ate		
stare		
stair		
see		
sea		

Overview

SUFFIXES EN AND ATE

flat	flatten
sweet	sweeten
tough	toughen
weak	weaken
awake	awaken
alien	alienate
elastic	elasticated
medicine	medicate

Spelling activity sheet

SET 13 SHEET B

NAME: ______________________________

Some nouns and adjectives can be changed to verbs by adding **ate** or **en**.

Take care – the spellings of some root words change at the end before the suffix is added.

Look in the word search for the root words from the following verbs. For example, the root word for 'alienate' is 'alien', so in the word search you are looking for 'alien'.

alienate medicate flatten toughen
elasticated sweeten awaken weaken

START

c	d	l	f	p	p	e	a	w	o	o	b	a	s	s	r
f	e	t	i	c	a	e	c	r	a	w	a	k	e	l	t
s	l	e	e	m	d	i	r	p	q	u	u	s	e	m	s
e	a	a	t	h	o	o	i	a	k	b	c	o	x	e	a
r	s	o	t	s	c	p	e	c	h	r	p	e	e	d	r
e	t	t	o	u	g	h	c	a	s	o	r	p	h	i	a
b	i	i	s	e	m	a	t	o	b	w	i	e	c	c	n
t	c	m	a	g	a	r	t	h	a	w	e	a	k	i	e
j	h	j	d	o	l	k	u	m	o	f	c	e	e	n	a
r	i	g	t	a	l	i	e	n	d	g	r	e	t	e	d

FINISH

Moving from left to right on each row, write down the letter in every fourth square. Begin on the square that is at the top left and finish on the eighth letter in the last row. You will have found four more words ending with 'ate'.

______________ ______________ ______________ ______________

Use a dictionary to help you to write a definition for each of your new words.

Learn, write, check

NAME: ____________________

Look and say	Write then cover	Write then check
flat		
flatten		
sweet		
sweeten		
tough		
toughen		
weak		
weaken		
awake		
awaken		
alien		
alienate		
elastic		
elasticated		
medicine		
medicate		

special	specialise
theory	theorise
personal	personalise
apology	apologise
real	realise
note	notify
jolly	jollify
pure	purify

Spelling activity sheet

NAME: ______________________________

Some nouns and adjectives can be made into verbs.

One way of doing this is by adding **ise** or **ify** to them.

Change the following words into verbs by adding 'ise' or 'ify'.
Remember you may need to change an e or a y at the end of a word into an i.

	ise
theory	______
personal	______
special	______
apology	______

	ify
note	______
pure	______
beauty	______
jolly	______

Now put your words into interesting sentences.

____
____
____
____
____
____
____
____
____
____

Try to write a sentence for each of the following words:

apologise   notify   personalised   classify   realise

Learn, write, check

NAME: 

Look and say	Write then cover	Write then check
special		
specialise		
theory		
theorise		
personal		
personalise		
apology		
apologise		
real		
realise		
note		
notify		
jolly		
jollify		
pure		
purify		

Overview

COMPOUND WORDS

outside	sometimes
without	birthday
something	someone
somewhere	somehow
cupboard	blackboard
fireplace	footwear
anything	everybody
beforehand	another

Spelling activity sheet

NAME: ______________________________

A compound word is made when two or more smaller words are put together.

Knowing this may help you to spell some of these words.

These twenty single words can be joined to make ten compound words.

out	dust	any	pan	board
shine	sauce	nut	hand	thing
an	other	cup	bin	sun
some	bag	chest	side	times

Can you find the compound words? Write them down in the spaces below.

______________ ______________ ______________ ______________

______________ ______________ ______________ ______________

______________ ______________

Complete these compound word chains. The first one is done for you.

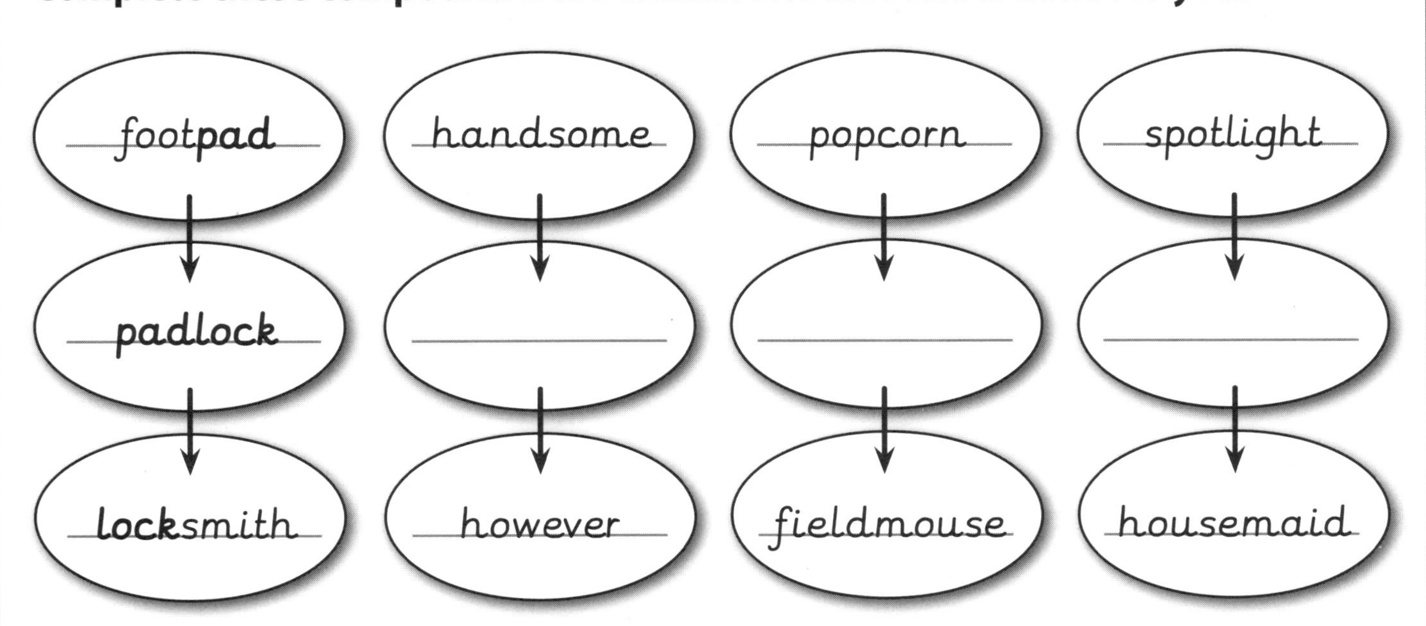

Try to find twenty more compound words. Use a dictionary to help you.

Learn, write, check

NAME: ______________________________

Look and say	Write then cover	Write then check
outside		
sometimes		
without		
birthday		
something		
someone		
somewhere		
somehow		
cupboard		
blackboard		
fireplace		
footwear		
anything		
everybody		
beforehand		
another		

SUFFIX LY

sudden	suddenly
second	secondly
hope	hoping
hopeful	hopefully
decorate	decorative
decoratively	wonderful
wonderfully	beauty
beautiful	beautifully

Spelling activity sheet

NAME: ______________________________

Extending a word changes how we use it in a sentence.

Extending an adjective by adding **ly** can change it into an adverb.

Choose which form of each of the words in the box is best in the sentence.

decorate	decorative	decoratively

I am going to ____________ my room with colourful posters.

hope	hoping	hopeful	hopefully

'____________,' thought the sailor, 'I will not be seasick.'

beauty	beautiful	beautifully

The painting was considered to be a thing of great ____________.

There are lots of endings that can be used to extend words. Here are some examples:

able al ic tion ly ful fully less ment ist ant ity ness ive

Remember that sometimes we need to change part of a word to add an ending to it. For example, we lose the letter y from 'happy' to make the word 'happiness'. See how many extended words you can make from the words below.

wonder restore care

You may need a dictionary to help you!

Learn, write, check

NAME: ______________________________

Look and say	Write then cover	Write then check
sudden		
suddenly		
second		
secondly		
hope		
hoping		
hopeful		
hopefully		
decorate		
decorative		
decoratively		
wonderful		
wonderfully		
beauty		
beautiful		
beautifully		

possible	impossible
reversible	terrible
horrible	edible
responsible	indestructible
passable	impassable
laughable	enjoyable
valuable	breakable
agreeable	miserable

Spelling activity sheet

NAME: ______________________

We often meet the suffixes **ible** and **able**.

Remember: a suffix is a word ending.

Follow the clues to complete the words. If you do this correctly you will find a word down the left hand column, spelt using the first letter of all your answers. Use the words in the box to help you.

climbable	impossible	laughable	reversible	notable
enjoyable	indestructible	breakable	edible	drinkable

1. ______________ Not able to be done.
2. ______________ Worthy of note.
3. ______________ You can reach the top of this mountain.
4. ______________ Can be worn inside out.
5. ______________ Pleasurable.
6. ______________ Good to drink.
7. ______________ Cannot be broken.
8. ______________ You can destroy this.
9. ______________ Amusing/ridiculous.
10. ______________ This will not poison you.

The word that I found is ______________

For each letter of the alphabet, find a word with either the suffix 'ible' or 'able'. The first two have been done for you. Note: you will not find any words for x, y and z.

a → agreeable
b → breakable
c → ______________
d → ______________
e → ______________
f → ______________
g → ______________
h → ______________
i → ______________
j → ______________
k → ______________
l → ______________
m → ______________
n → ______________
o → ______________
p → ______________
q → ______________
r → ______________
s → ______________
t → ______________
u → ______________
v → ______________
w → ______________

Learn, write, check

NAME: ______________________

Look and say	Write then cover	Write then check
possible		
impossible		
reversible		
terrible		
horrible		
edible		
responsible		
indestructible		
passable		
impassable		
laughable		
enjoyable		
valuable		
breakable		
agreeable		
miserable		

SOUND I SPELT Y

myth	gym
Egypt	Egyptian
pyramid	mystery
mysteries	gymnast
gymnastics	gymnasium
mysterious	rhyme
rhythm	rhythmic
rhythmical	mythical

Spelling activity sheet

SET
18
SHEET
B

NAME: ______________________

Sometimes the letter **y** makes the sound **i**.

One word in the list does not have the **i** sound.

rhythmic	rhythm	gymnasium	rhythmical
Egyptian	myth	mysteries	gymnast
gymnastics	Egypt	gym	mystery
mysterious	mythical	pyramid	rhyme

Which word does not have the i sound? ______________________

Sort the words into sets.

Complete these sentences using the words at the top of the page.

1. I would like to go to ____________ to see a ____________.
2. The ____________ moved to the ____________ of the music during her floor routine.
3. I like books that have a ____________ story.

Write your own sentence using at least one of the words from the list.

____

____

Learn, write, check

NAME: ______________________

Look and say	Write then cover	Write then check
myth		
gym		
Egypt		
Egyptian		
pyramid		
mystery		
mysteries		
gymnast		
gymnastics		
gymnasium		
mysterious		
rhyme		
rhythm		
rhythmic		
rhythmical		
mythical		

Overview

PREFIXES IN AND IL

active	inactive
correct	incorrect
incorrectly	destruct
destructible	indestructible
competent	incompetent
legal	illegal
legible	illegible
logical	illogical

Spelling activity sheet

NAME: ______________________________

Some words can be changed into their opposites…

… just by adding **in** or **il**.

Choose whether to add 'in' or 'il' to the words on the left to change them into their opposites.

WORD	OPPOSITE
destructible	______
logical	______
correct	______
active	______
legal	______
competent	______
legible	______

Write the missing words in the sentences. You may need to use some of the opposites you have just written.

I couldn't read the letter because the writing was ______________.

The maths puzzle was easy because it was ______________.

Can you find the ______________ answer to the question?

We couldn't knock the wall down because it was ______________.

Write a sentence of your own using one of the words on the list.

____

____

Learn, write, check

NAME: ______________________

Look and say	Write then cover	Write then check
active		
inactive		
correct		
incorrect		
incorrectly		
destruct		
destructible		
indestructible		
competent		
incompetent		
legal		
illegal		
legible		
illegible		
logical		
illogical		

regular	irregular
relevant	irrelevant
removable	irremovable
responsible	irresponsible
septic	antiseptic
clockwise	anticlockwise
social	antisocial
climax	anticlimax

NAME: ______________________________

Some words can be changed into their opposites…

… just by adding **ir** or **anti**.

Choose whether to add 'ir' or 'anti' to the words on the left to change them into their opposites.

WORD	OPPOSITE
clockwise	____________
removable	____________
regular	____________
responsible	____________
climax	____________
relevant	____________
social	____________
septic	____________

Write the missing words in the sentences. You may need to use some of the opposites you have just written.

The water went down the drain in an ____________ direction.

I was very pleased that the sticky label was ____________.

Who is ____________ for the marvellous display of pictures?

The football result was 0-0, which was a bit of an ____________.

Write a sentence of your own using one of the words on the list.

____

____

Learn, write, check

NAME: ______________________

Look and say	Write then cover	Write then check
regular		
irregular		
relevant		
irrelevant		
removable		
irremovable		
responsible		
irresponsible		
septic		
antiseptic		
clockwise		
anticlockwise		
social		
antisocial		
climax		
anticlimax		

Overview

PREFIXES INTER AND SUB

act	interact
city	intercity
national	international
related	interrelated
heading	subheading
merge	submerge
marine	submarine
network	internet

Spelling activity sheet

NAME: ______________________

The prefix **inter** means **between**…

… and the prefix **sub** means under or beneath.

Follow the clues to fill in the word hexagon.
Use the words in the box to help you.

city
submarine
international
submerge
internet
intercity

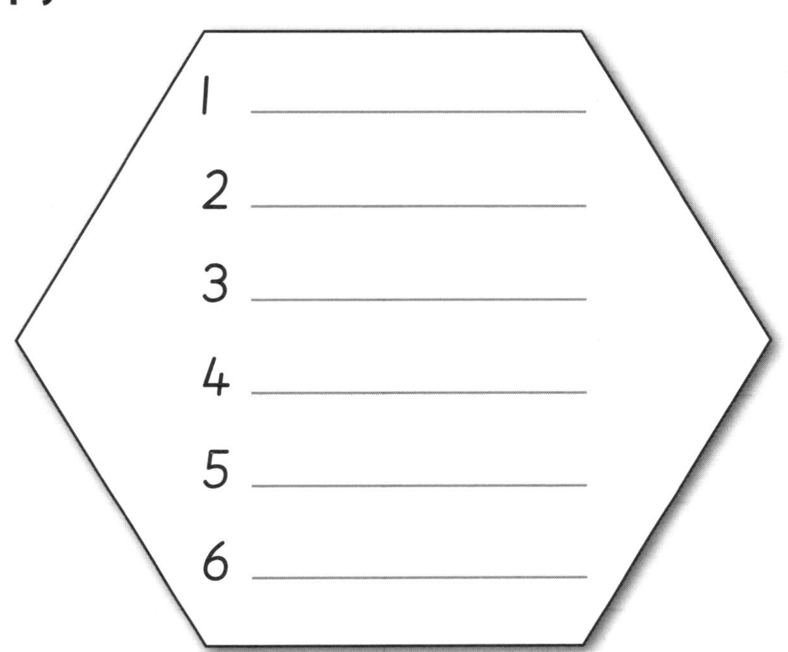

CLUES:

1. usually a very big town, often having a cathedral
2. to go underneath the water
3. between countries
4. a ship for travelling under the surface of the sea
5. between cities
6. used for communication through computers

Write a definition for each of the following words. Use a dictionary to help you.

merge ______________________

act ______________________

national ______________________

heading ______________________

Learn, write, check

NAME: ____________________

Look and say	Write then cover	Write then check
act		
interact		
city		
intercity		
national		
international		
related		
interrelated		
heading		
subheading		
merge		
submerge		
marine		
submarine		
network		
internet		

graph	autograph
pilot	autopilot
mobile	automobile
immobile	mobility
biography	autobiography
focus	autofocus
automate	automatic
automation	automatically

Spelling activity sheet

SET 22 SHEET B

NAME: ______________________________

The prefix **im** changes words to their opposites…

… but the prefix **auto** is related to 'self' or 'one's own' or 'by itself'.

graph | autograph | pilot | autopilot | mobile | automobile

immobile | mobility | immobility | biography | autobiography | focus

autofocus | automatic | automatically

Choose a word to fill each gap.

She was driving along in a very smart

________________.

The maths teacher asked me to draw a

________________.

I asked the singer for his ________________.

It was quite difficult to ________________ my old camera but my new one has ________________.

When I'm older I'd quite like to be a

________________.

Which is the only word on the list that can have both the prefixes?

____

Use a dictionary to help you to write a definition for these words.

automobile ____

immobile ____

Learn, write, check

NAME: ____________________

Look and say	Write then cover	Write then check
graph		
autograph		
pilot		
autopilot		
mobile		
automobile		
immobile		
mobility		
biography		
autobiography		
focus		
autofocus		
automate		
automatic		
automation		
automatically		

Overview

ADDING SUFFIXES, AND WORDS BEGINNING INTER

arrive	arriving
arrived	arrival
occasion	occasional
occasionally	advent
invent	invention
prevent	prevention
interact	interfere
intervene	interrupt

Spelling activity sheet

NAME: ______________________________

Lots of words are related to each other.

How many words can you think of that are related to the word **arrive**?

arrived	arrive	arrival	prevention
interfere	interrupt	prevent	advent
occasional	invent	interact	occasion
invention	occasionally	intervene	arriving

Sort the words into sets. It's not easy!

______	______	______	______
______	______	______	______
______	______	______	______
______		______	______
		______	

Now write the missing words in these sentences.

1. My mum's birthday was a wonderful ______________.
2. The ______________ of the train was delayed by ten minutes.
3. It's important to try to ______________ accidents.

Write your own sentence using at least one of the words from the list.

____

____

Learn, write, check

NAME: ______________________

Look and say	Write then cover	Write then check
arrive		
arriving		
arrived		
arrival		
occasion		
occasional		
occasionally		
advent		
invent		
invention		
prevent		
prevention		
interact		
interfere		
intervene		
interrupt		

humble	humbly
noble	nobly
regular	regularly
basic	basically
frantic	frantically
dramatic	dramatically
music	musically
magic	magically

Spelling activity sheet

NAME: ______________________________

When a word ends with **le**, you can replace it with **ly**.

When a word ends with **al**, you can add **ly** to it.

Look:

crumble ⟶ crumbly

musical ⟶ musically

Add 'ly', 'al' or 'ally' to each of these words to make new words.

humble → ______ magical → ______

noble → ______ dramatic → ______

rumple → ______ fantastic → ______

bubble → ______ quizzical → ______

wrinkle → ______ basic → ______

tangle → ______ rhythmical → ______

single → ______ frantic → ______

Use a dictionary to help you to write a definition for each of the following words.

rhythmical ______________________________

dramatically ______________________________

wrinkly ______________________________

Learn, write, check

NAME: ______________________

Look and say	Write then cover	Write then check
humble		
humbly		
noble		
nobly		
regular		
regularly		
basic		
basically		
frantic		
frantically		
dramatic		
dramatically		
music		
musically		
magic		
magically		

Overview

CREATING WORDS FROM OTHERS

true	truly
truth	truthful
truthfulness	due
duly	overdue
duration	durable
endure	endurable
unendurable	whole
wholly	wholesome

Spelling activity sheet

NAME: ______________________________

Do you think we've found all the words derived from the root word true?
I can think of another!

Look at these words

true truly truth truthful truthfulness

One of these words can have an extra suffix added.
Find the word and create a new word by adding a suffix.

______________ ⟶ ______________

All of these words, including the new one, can be changed to their opposites by adding the prefix 'un':

true → ______________
truly → ______________
truth → ______________
truthful → ______________
truthfulness → ______________

Write three sentences, using at least one of the words from the box in each one.

due	duration	endurable	wholly
duly	durable	unendurable	wholesome
overdue	endure	whole	

Learn, write, check

NAME: ______________________

Look and say	Write then cover	Write then check
true		
truly		
truth		
truthful		
truthfulness		
due		
duly		
overdue		
duration		
durable		
endure		
endurable		
unendurable		
whole		
wholly		
wholesome		

Overview

ENDING SION WITH J SOUND SPELT S; WORDS WITH V

divide	division
invade	invasion
confuse	confusion
decide	decision
collide	collision
televise	television
favour	favourite
flavour	develop

NAME: ______________________

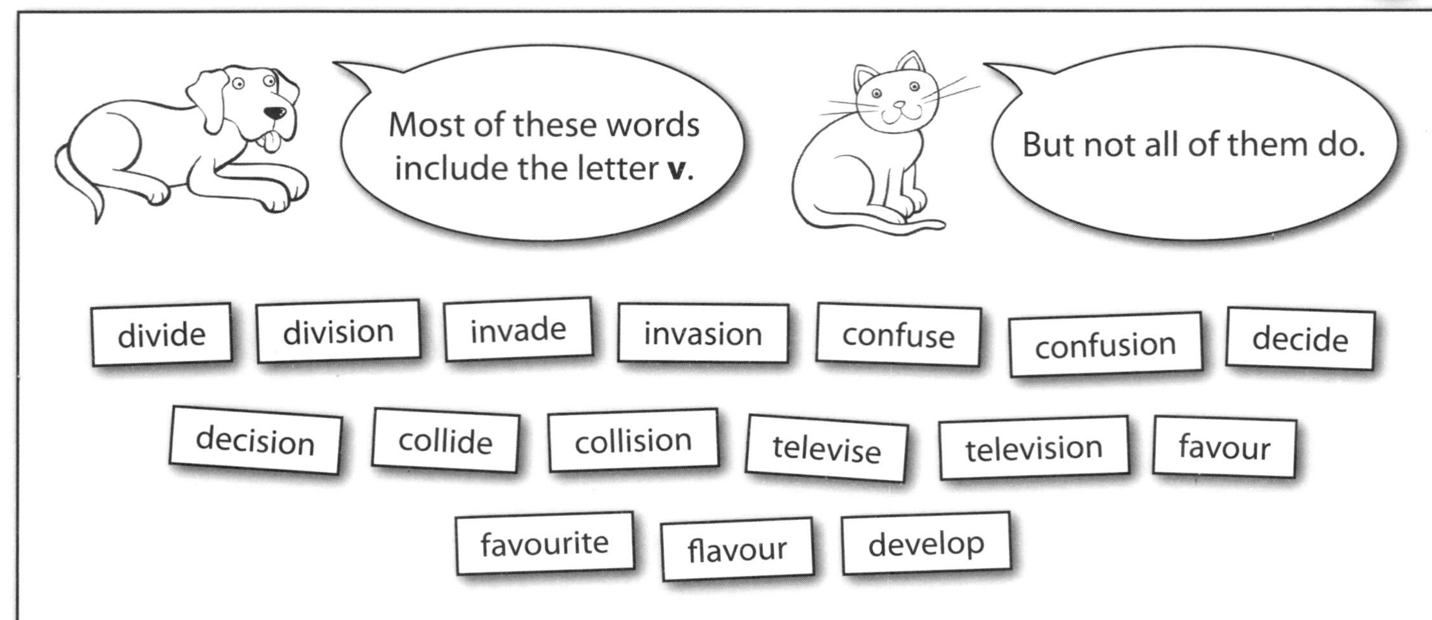

Sort the words to fit into the Venn diagram. Some words will go in the left ring. Some words will go in the right ring. Some words will go in both rings so write them where the rings overlap. Some words will not go in the rings at all so they need to be written around the edge.

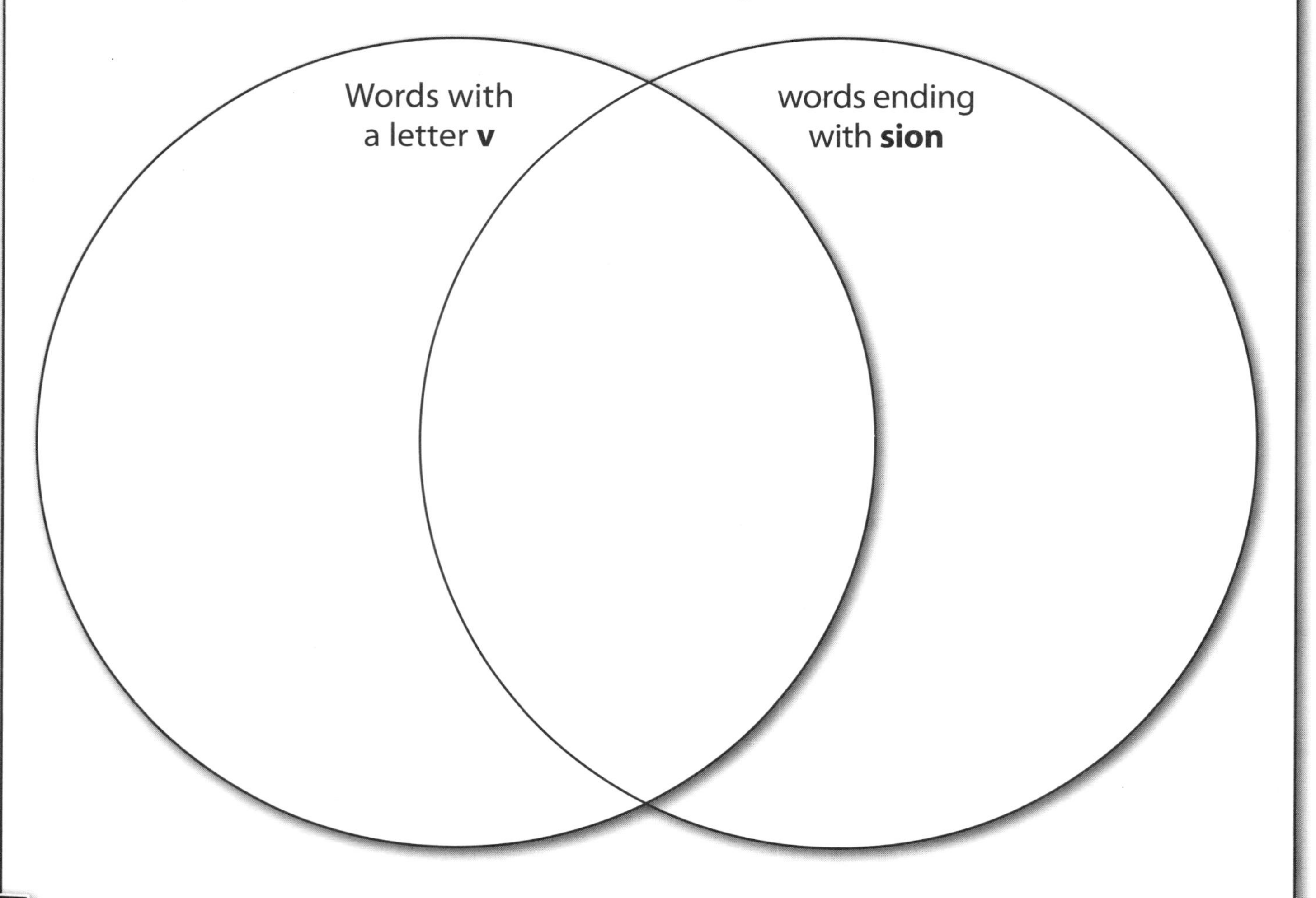

Learn, write, check

NAME: ______________________

Look and say	Write then cover	Write then check
divide		
division		
invade		
invasion		
confuse		
confusion		
decide		
decision		
collide		
collision		
televise		
television		
favour		
favourite		
flavour		
develop		

humour	humorous
glamour	glamorous
vigour	vigorous
courage	courageous
outrage	outrageous
serious	obvious
curious	hideous
spontaneous	courteous

Spelling activity sheet

NAME: ______________________

Have you noticed how some words need to be changed…

…when adding the suffix **ous**?

Sort the words into sets.

humour	vigour	outrage	curious	flavour
humorous	vigorous	outrageous	hideous	favour
glamour	courage	serious	spontaneous	
glamorous	courageous	obvious	courteous	

Words ending **our**	Words ending **ous**	Words ending **age**

Can you add some extra words to the box of words ending 'age'?

Write four sentences, each one containing at least one of the words from the word bank.

Learn, write, check

SET 27 SHEET C

NAME: ______________________

Look and say	Write then cover	Write then check
humour		
humorous		
glamour		
glamorous		
vigour		
vigorous		
courage		
courageous		
outrage		
outrageous		
serious		
obvious		
curious		
hideous		
spontaneous		
courteous		

ENDINGS SION, SIVE AND TION

expand	expansion
expansive	extend
extension	extensive
comprehend	comprehension
comprehensive	tend
tension	attend
attention	intend
intention	pretend

Spelling activity sheet

NAME: ______________________________

Have you noticed how the **d** from **comprehend** is changed to an **s** when **ion** is added?

But the **d** from **attend** is changed to a **t** when **ion** is added!

Sort the words into sets.

expand	extension	comprehensive	attention
expansion	extensive	tend	intend
expansive	comprehend	tension	intention
extend	comprehension	attend	pretend

Words ending **and**

Words ending **end**

Words ending **sion**

Words ending **tion**

Words ending **sive**

Can you add some extra words to the boxes to fill them up?

Learn, write, check

NAME: ______________________

Look and say	Write then cover	Write then check
expand		
expansion		
expansive		
extend		
extension		
extensive		
comprehend		
comprehension		
comprehensive		
tend		
tension		
attend		
attention		
intend		
intention		
pretend		

Overview

ENDINGS CIAN AND AL

music	musician
musical	musically
electric	electrician
electrical	magic
magician	magical
magically	politics
politician	mathematics
mathematician	mathematical

Spelling activity sheet

NAME: ____________________

We've seen some of these words before.

It's good to revise them!

Look at the words below and study their suffixes and prefixes.

music	electric	magician	politician
musician	electrician	magical	mathematics
musical	electrical	magically	mathematician
musically	magic	politics	mathematical

Here are some extra root words that can be altered or extended using suffixes or prefixes.

logic medicine tradition chemistry season

Try to find some words that are related to the root words. The words in the box at the top of this page may give you some clues. You can also use a dictionary to help you.

logic

____
____
____
____

medicine

____
____
____
____

tradition

____
____
____
____

chemistry

____
____
____
____

season

____
____
____
____

NAME: ______________________

Look and say	Write then cover	Write then check
music		
musician		
musical		
musically		
electric		
electrician		
electrical		
magic		
magician		
magical		
magically		
politics		
politician		
mathematics		
mathematician		
mathematical		

MICRO AND MINI

microscope	microbe
micron	microphone
minibus	minibeast
minicab	miniature
minimum	minimise
little	minor
small	tiny
petite	minute

Spelling activity sheet

SET 30 SHEET B

NAME: ____________________

Mini is a word root that means small.

Micro also means small.

Fill in the blanks in the sentences below.
The words you will need are all in the box.

microphone	microbe	minibus	microscope
miniature	minimum	minibeasts	

1. I would use a ______________ to look at a ______________.
2. She sang into the ______________.
3. Look under a large stone to find some ______________.
4. Ten people went out in a ______________.
5. Seventeen is the ______________ age at which you can drive a car on the road.
6. A ______________ poodle is a very small breed of dog.

Make a list of all the words you can find connected with small things and a list of words to do with large things (e.g. 'huge', 'gigantic', etc.).

SMALL	LARGE

Learn, write, check

NAME: ______________________

Look and say	Write then cover	Write then check
microscope		
microbe		
micron		
microphone		
minibus		
minibeast		
minicab		
miniature		
minimum		
minimise		
little		
minor		
small		
tiny		
petite		
minute		

scheme	chorus
choir	choral
chemist	chemistry
chemical	echo
character	science
scientist	scientific
scene	discipline
fascinate	crescent

Spelling activity sheet

NAME: ______________________________

Listen to the sound **ch** makes in the word choir.

And the sound **sc** makes in scene.

scheme	chemist	character	scene
chorus	chemistry	science	discipline
choir	chemical	scientist	fascinate
choral	echo	scientific	crescent

Use words from the word bank to fill the gaps in the passage below.

My sister does three ______________ subjects at her school; they are biology, physics and ______________. She says she wants to be a ______________ when she grows up. She also likes singing, so last year she joined the school ______________. At Christmas she was in the school play, and in one ______________ she had to sing a solo then everybody else joined in for the ______________. I can't remember the name of the ______________ she played but she had to wear a really nice costume.

Which words from the word bank did you not use?

______________ ______________ ______________

______________ ______________ ______________

______________ ______________ ______________

Write a sentence using at least one of the words you did not use.

____

____

Learn, write, check

NAME: ______________________

Look and say	Write then cover	Write then check
scheme		
chorus		
choir		
choral		
chemist		
chemistry		
chemical		
echo		
character		
science		
scientist		
scientific		
scene		
discipline		
fascinate		
crescent		

Overview

APOSTROPHES TO SHOW POSSESSION

girl's	boy's
baby's	lady's
girls'	boys'
babies'	ladies'
children's	men's
women's	mice's
Cyprus's	James's
Chris's	Jess's

Spelling activity sheet

NAME: ______________________________

You need to know how to use apostrophes.

Read the clues very carefully.

Apostrophes are used when letters are missed out. Look:

cannot ⟶ can't   it is ⟶ it's

Apostrophes are also used to show ownership. Just remember, the apostrophe comes after the owner or owners. Look:

Here is the dog's dinner.

One dog: the dog's dinner

If there is more than one owner, the apostrophe goes after the plural s. Look:

Here are the dogs' dinners.

Two dogs: the dogs' dinners

But look at this:

Here are the children's dinners.

Three children: the children's dinners

The apostrophe came before the s, because the word 'children' is already plural.

Write a sentence about a teddy belonging to a baby.

____

____

Write a sentence about some scooters belonging to two girls.

____

____

Write a sentence about some books belonging to two babies.

____

____

Write a sentence about some stickers belonging to a boy.

____

____

Write a sentence about a bike belonging to a girl.

____

____

Write a sentence about a canoe shared by two boys.

____

____

Learn, write, check

NAME: ______________________

Look and say	Write then cover	Write then check
girl's		
boy's		
baby's		
lady's		
girls'		
boys'		
babies'		
ladies'		
children's		
men's		
women's		
mice's		
Cyprus's		
James's		
Chris's		
Jess's		

WORD LIST FOR YEARS 3 AND 4

actual	bicycle
calendar	disappear
extreme	grammar
increase	mention
notice	position
probably	straight
therefore	various
whose	woman

NAME: ______________________

How do you put words into alphabetical order if they both start with the same letter?

You have to look at the second letter.

Look carefully at the words in the word bank. Some words have the same first letter.

straight | calendar | mention | probably | bicycle | woman
extreme | whose | therefore | disappear | notice | actual | various
increase | position | grammar

Write the words in alphabetical order.

______ ______ ______ ______

______ ______ ______ ______

______ ______ ______ ______

______ ______ ______ ______

Write a sentence that includes three of the words from the word bank.

______

______

______

One of the words already has the suffix 'ly'. Which other words could have the suffix 'ly' added to them? Write the words then write the new words with 'ly' added.

______ → ______

______ → ______

______ → ______

______ → ______

Learn, write, check

NAME: ______________________

Look and say	Write then cover	Write then check
actual		
bicycle		
calendar		
disappear		
extreme		
grammar		
increase		
mention		
notice		
position		
probably		
straight		
therefore		
various		
whose		
woman		

Overview

WORD LIST FOR YEARS 3 AND 4

accident	breath
caught	century
describe	eight
famous	group
height	important
knowledge	library
minute	occasion
ordinary	perhaps

Spelling activity sheet

NAME: ______________________________

How many times does the letter **r** appear in **library**?

I thought there was only one **r**, but there are two!

Look carefully at the words in the word bank. Some words have the same first letter.

describe	famous	perhaps	library	accident	century
occasion	important	breath	group	ordinary	eight
knowledge	caught	minute	height		

Write the words in alphabetical order.

______________ ______________ ______________ ______________

______________ ______________ ______________ ______________

______________ ______________ ______________ ______________

______________ ______________ ______________ ______________

Write a sentence that includes three of the words from the word bank.

____

____

____

One of the words already has the suffix 'ly'. Which other words could have the suffix 'ly' added to them? Some of the words will need to have the suffix 'al' added before you can add 'ly'. One word will need its final letter y changed to a letter i before adding 'ly'. Write the words then write the new words with 'ly' added.

______________ ⟶ ______________

______________ ⟶ ______________

______________ ⟶ ______________

______________ ⟶ ______________

______________ ⟶ ______________

______________ ⟶ ______________

Learn, write, check

NAME: ______________________

Look and say	Write then cover	Write then check
accident		
breath		
caught		
century		
describe		
eight		
famous		
group		
height		
important		
knowledge		
library		
minute		
occasion		
ordinary		
perhaps		

Overview

WORD LIST FOR YEARS 3 AND 4

actually	breathe
centre	different
exercise	fruit
heart	island
naughty	particular
promise	remember
strength	through
weather	weigh

Spelling activity sheet

NAME:

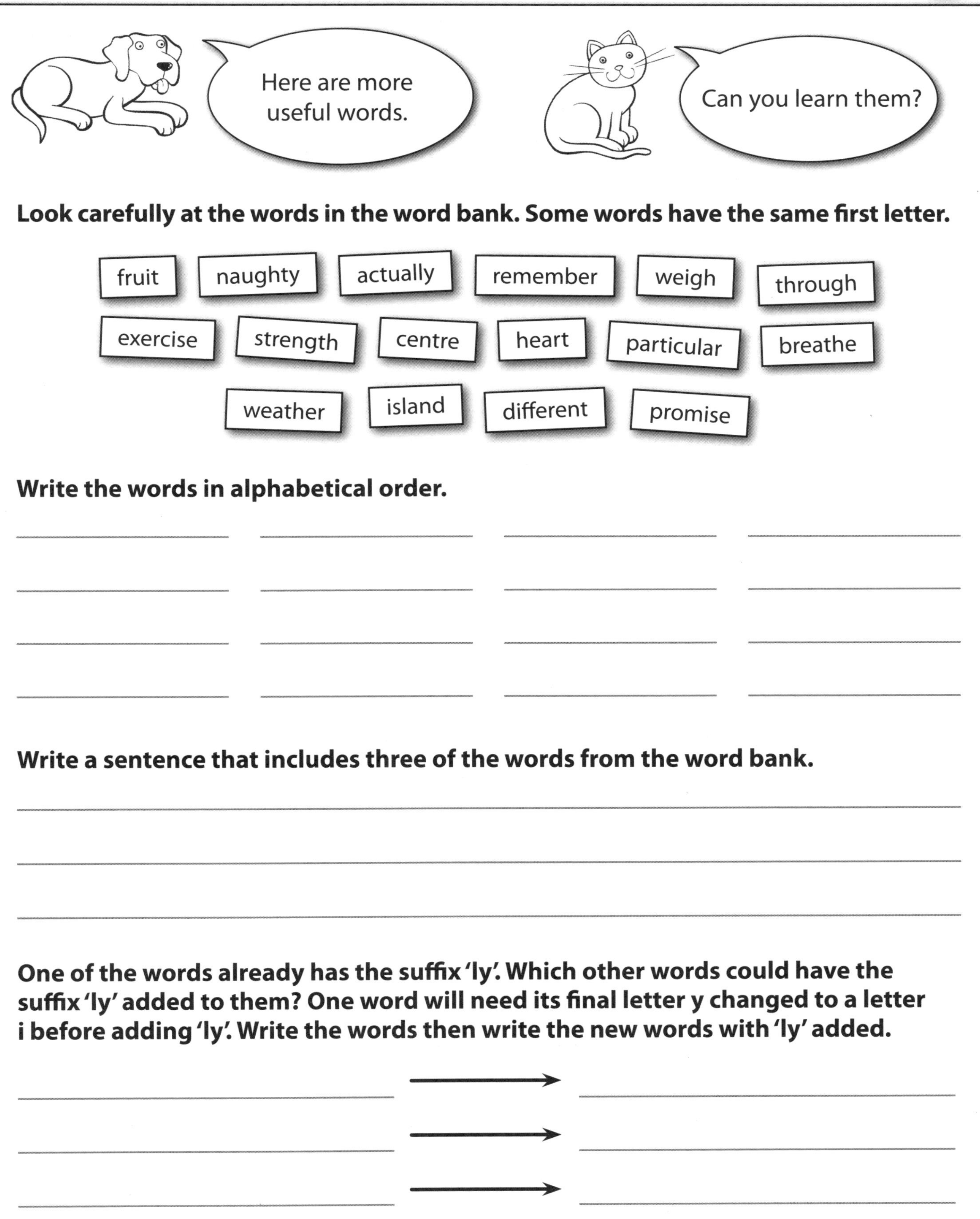

Here are more useful words.
Can you learn them?

Look carefully at the words in the word bank. Some words have the same first letter.

fruit | naughty | actually | remember | weigh | through
exercise | strength | centre | heart | particular | breathe
weather | island | different | promise

Write the words in alphabetical order.

Write a sentence that includes three of the words from the word bank.

One of the words already has the suffix 'ly'. Which other words could have the suffix 'ly' added to them? One word will need its final letter y changed to a letter i before adding 'ly'. Write the words then write the new words with 'ly' added.

Learn, write, check

NAME: ______________________________

Look and say	Write then cover	Write then check
actually		
breathe		
centre		
different		
exercise		
fruit		
heart		
island		
naughty		
particular		
promise		
remember		
strength		
through		
weather		
weigh		

Overview

WORD LIST FOR YEARS 3 AND 4

accidentally	believe
circle	earth
favourite	guard
imagine	medicine
occasionally	potatoes
quarter	reign
separate	surprise
although	who's

Spelling activity sheet

NAME: ____________________

It's surprising how you spell **surprise**!

Lots of these words have unusual spellings.

Look carefully at the words in the word bank. Some words have the same first letter.

reign | medicine | guard | accidentally | favourite | imagine

who's | earth | believe | potatoes | quarter | surprise

circle | occasionally | although | separate

Write the words in alphabetical order.

____	____	____	____
____	____	____	____
____	____	____	____
____	____	____	____

Look at this word: believe

Here are some other words that are related to believe:

belief beliefs believer believing believed

For each word shown below, try to find other words that are related.

medicine	favourite	imagine	surprise
____	____	____	____
____	____	____	____
____	____	____	____
____	____	____	____

Learn, write, check

SET 36 SHEET C

NAME: ______________________

Look and say	Write then cover	Write then check
accidentally		
believe		
circle		
earth		
favourite		
guard		
imagine		
medicine		
occasionally		
potatoes		
quarter		
reign		
separate		
surprise		
although		
who's		

Overview

WORD LIST FOR YEARS 3 AND 4

address	build
certain	decide
experience	February
guide	history
learn	natural
pressure	question
recent	sentence
though	whether

NAME: ______________________

February is the second month of the year.

It's also the shortest month.

Look carefully at the words in the word bank. Some words have the same first letter.

though | February | certain | question | build | natural

history | whether | address | guide | pressure | sentence

experience | learn | decide | recent

Write the words in alphabetical order.

______ ______ ______ ______

______ ______ ______ ______

______ ______ ______ ______

______ ______ ______ ______

Look at this rhyme:

Thirty days has September, April, June and November.
All the rest have thirty-one, except February,
Which has twenty-eight days clear
And twenty-nine each leap year.

Write the twelve months of the year in order. Use the rhyme to help you also write down the number of days in each month. January and February have been done for you.

January 31 ______ ______

February 28 or 29 ______ ______

______ ______ ______

______ ______ ______

Learn, write, check

NAME: ______________________________

Look and say	Write then cover	Write then check
address		
build		
certain		
decide		
experience		
February		
guide		
history		
learn		
natural		
pressure		
question		
recent		
sentence		
though		
whether		

WORD LIST FOR YEARS 3 AND 4

answer	busy
complete	consider
difficult	early
forward	heard
length	material
often	popular
possess	special
suppose	weight

Spelling activity sheet

NAME: ______________________________

Have you noticed there's a **w** in the word **answer**?

And have you noticed that the letter **u** sounds like **i** in the word **busy**?

Look carefully at the words in the word bank. Some words have the same first letter.

special | difficult | answer | material | possess | forward

weight | consider | busy | early | popular | length

heard | complete | often | suppose

Write the words in alphabetical order.

______	______	______	______
______	______	______	______
______	______	______	______
______	______	______	______

Write some related words for each of the words below.
The first one has been done for you.

special → speciality
special → especially
special → specialism

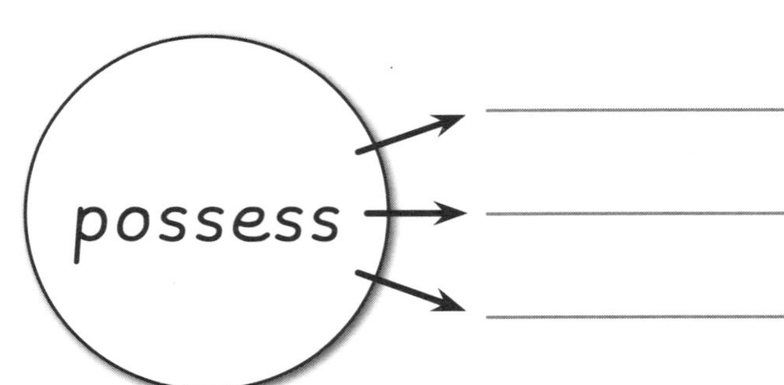

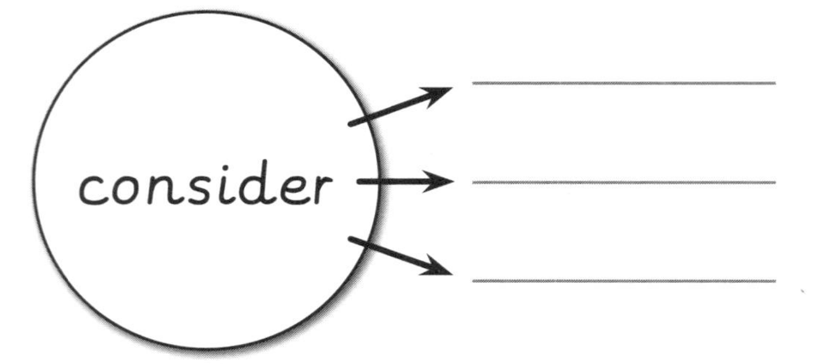

Learn, write, check

NAME: ____________________

Look and say	Write then cover	Write then check
answer		
busy		
complete		
consider		
difficult		
early		
forward		
heard		
length		
material		
often		
popular		
possess		
special		
suppose		
weight		

Overview

WORD LIST FOR YEARS 3 AND 4

appear	business
continue	eighth
enough	experiment
forwards	interest
opposite	peculiar
possession	purpose
regular	strange
thought	women

Spelling activity sheet

NAME: ______________________

Have you noticed that you can't hear the **i** in **business**?

And have you noticed that the letter **o** sounds like **i** in the word women?

Look carefully at the words in the word bank. Some words have the same first letter.

purpose	women	business	forwards	opposite	regular
appear	enough	possession	interest	eighth	strange
continue	experiment	peculiar	thought		

Write the words in alphabetical order.

Write some related words for each of the words below.
The first one has been done for you.

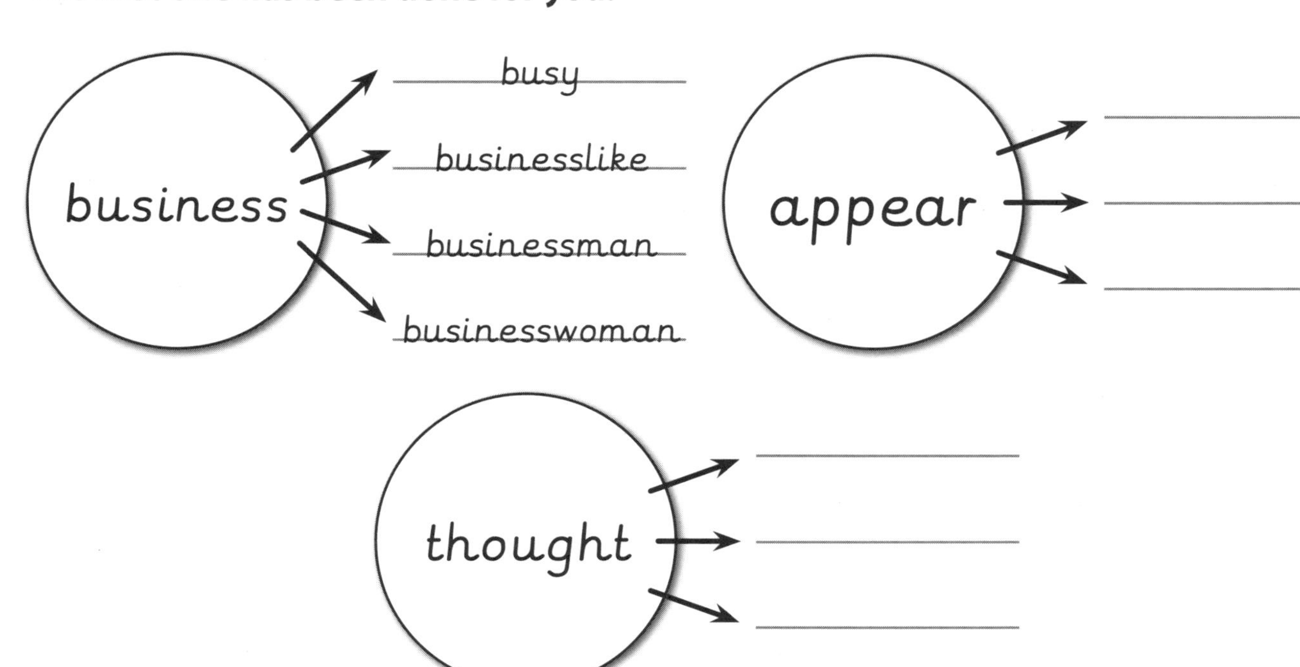

Learn, write, check

NAME: ______________________________

Look and say	Write then cover	Write then check
appear		
business		
continue		
eighth		
enough		
experiment		
forwards		
interest		
opposite		
peculiar		
possession		
purpose		
regular		
strange		
thought		
women		

Overview

UNUSUAL SUFFIXES

brotherhood	knighthood
livelihood	neighbourhood
childhood	falsehood
friendship	membership
relationship	hardship
companionship	partnership
workmanship	craftsmanship
companionship	ownership

Spelling activity sheet

NAME: ______________________________

The suffixes **hood** and **ship** are often found on the ends of words.

Remember, if a word ends in **y**, change it to **i** before adding **ship** or **hood**.

Add the correct suffix to each of these words.

brother →	brotherhood	champion →	______
knight →	______	lively →	______
friend →	______	child →	______
neighbour →	______	owner →	______
relation →	______	partner →	______

Follow the clues to find a friendly word with a suffix down the middle of this puzzle.

Clues:

1. feline
2. bed for a baby
3. a morsel
4. a teapot has one
5. do this to potatoes
6. opposite of over
7. opposite of out
8. canine
9. spend this
10. travel on this
11. lives in water
12. a light fog
13. opposite of down

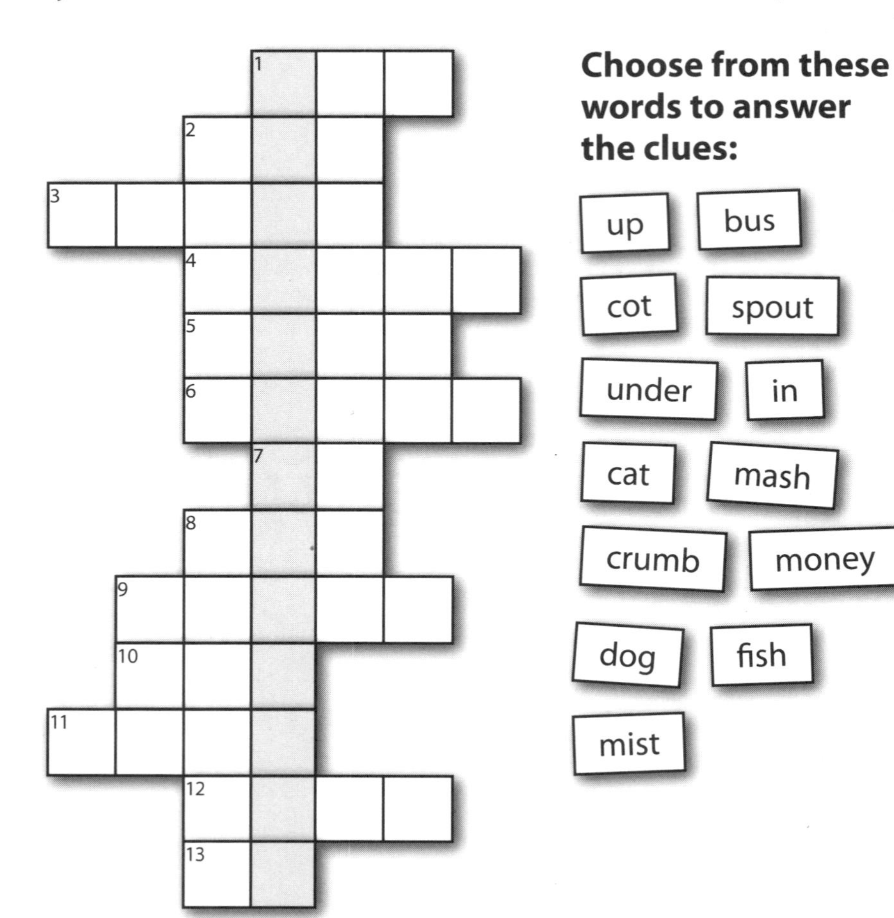

Work with a partner to see how many words you can find ending with 'hood' or 'ship'.

Learn, write, check

NAME: ____________________

Look and say	Write then cover	Write then check
brotherhood		
knighthood		
livelihood		
neighbourhood		
childhood		
falsehood		
friendship		
membership		
relationship		
hardship		
companionship		
partnership		
workmanship		
craftsmanship		
companionship		
ownership		

Answers

Set 1 Sheet B, p7

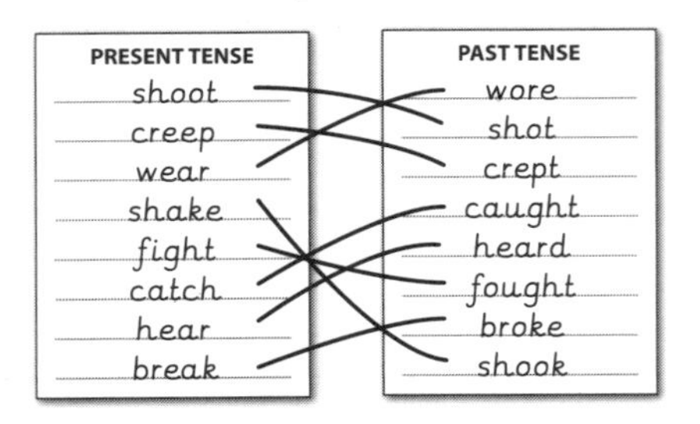

Set 2 Sheet B, p10

calves
halves
leaves
knives
wolves
gloves

Examples of words ending in ff: fluff bluff off cliff puff stuff muff gruff cuff staff ruff scruff scuff sheriff sniff stiff

Set 3 Sheet B, p13

tion words: station competition action subtraction reaction ration information question
ious words: obvious ferocious suspicious serious glorious previous curious atrocious delicious

Set 4 Sheet B, p16

also
alone
almost
already
although
altogether

alarm: a warning of danger
always: at all times
allure: attractiveness
allot: give a share of something

Set 5 Sheet B, p19

adopt
admire
advance
addition
adventure
adjust
address
adverb
adapt

admit: agree something is true
adjust: put in the correct postition
adjoin: be next to and joined with
advert: an advertisement

Set 6 Sheet B, p22

assortment, affectionate, attend, attractive, assemble

affirm: state a fact strongly
attend: be present at
affix: fasten or attach
affliction: pain or illness

Set 7 Sheet B, p25

alone	again	flight	special
attract	avenue	enough	correction
aloft	admire	bright	subtraction
ascend	through	suspicious	station

Possible extra words for each box:

after	addition	tight	invention
attitude	absolutely	cough	envious
afraid	advance	sight	attention
Africa	advise	rough	precious

Set 8 Sheet B, p28

its, it's, It's, its, It's

expensive, active, captive, massive, relative, competitive

Set 9 Sheet B, p31

autumn, aunt, favourite, route, ground, through, thought, sausage, poured, ground, journey, because, trousers

Set 10 Sheet B, p34

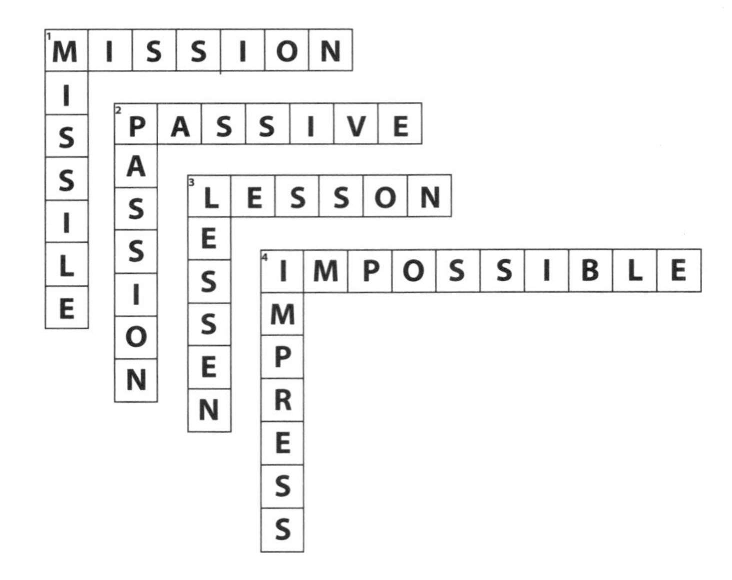

Set 11 Sheet B, p37

merriness
sadness
darkness
engagement
hardness
kindness
entertainment
government
silliness
drowsiness
endearment
softness
happiness
agreement
appointment
enjoyment

endearment: an expression of affection
government: a group of people governing the state
appointment: an arrangement to meet at a specific time

Set 12 Sheet B, p40

Pupil draws pictures in boxes and composes sentences.

Set 13 Sheet B, p43

c	d	l	f	p	p	e	a	w	o	o	b	a	s	s	r
f	e	t	i	c	a	e	c	r	a	w	a	k	e	l	t
s	l	e	e	m	d	i	r	p	q	u	u	s	e	m	s
e	a	a	t	h	o	o	i	a	k	b	c	o	x	e	a
r	s	o	t	s	c	p	e	c	h	r	p	e	e	d	r
e	t	t	o	u	g	h	c	a	s	o	r	p	h	i	a
b	i	i	s	e	m	a	t	o	b	w	i	e	c	c	n
t	c	m	a	g	a	r	t	h	a	w	e	a	k	i	e
j	h	j	d	o	l	k	u	m	o	f	c	e	e	n	a
r	i	g	t	a	l	i	e	n	d	g	r	e	t	e	d

fabricate rusticate procrastinate educate

Set 14 Sheet B, p46

theorise specialise personalise apologise notify beautify purify jollify

Set 15 Sheet B, p49

outside dustbin anything cupboard sunshine saucepan chestnut another sometimes handbag

somehow cornfield lighthouse

Set 16 Sheet B, p52

decorate
Hopefully
beauty

wondering wondered wonderful wonderfully wonderland wonderment
restoring restored restoration restorative restorable
caring cared careful carefully careless carelessly carelessness carer

Set 17 Sheet B, p55

impossible
notable
climbable
reversible
enjoyable
drinkable
indestructible
breakable
laughable
edible

incredible

capable dependable eligible feasible gullible horrible impressionable justifiable knowledgeable likeable movable noticeable operable pleasurable questionable reliable suitable terrible unbelievable veritable workable x - y - z –

Set 18 Sheet B, p58

rhyme
rhythmic
rhythm
rhythmical
rhyme
gymnasium
gymnast
gymnastics
gym
Egyptian
Egypt
pyramid
myth
mythical
mysteries
mystery
mysterious

Missing words: Egypt, pyramid gymnast, rhythm mystery

Set 19 Sheet B, p61

indestructible
illogical
incorrect
inactive
illegal
incompetent
illegible

Missing words: illegible logical correct indestructible

Set 20 Sheet B, p64

anticlockwise
irremovable
irregular
irresponsible
anticlimax
irrelevant
antisocial
antiseptic

Missing words: anticlockwise removable responsible anticlimax

Set 21 Sheet B, p67

city
submerge
international
submarine
intercity
internet

merge: combine
act: perform as a character
national: related to a country
heading: title

Set 22 Sheet B, p70

automobile graph autograph focus autofocus pilot mobile
automobile: a car with an engine
immobile: not movable

Set 23 Sheet B, p73

arrive	occasion	prevent	intefere
arrival	occasional	prevention	interrupt
arrived	occasionally	invent	interact
arriving		invention	intervene
		advent	

Missing words: occasion arrival prevent

Set 24 Sheet B, p76

humbly	magically
nobly	dramatically
rumply	fantastically
bubbly	quizzically
wrinkly	basically
tangly	rhythmically
singly	frantically

rhythmical: with rhythm
dramatically: with drama, suddenly or excitedly
wrinkly: with wrinkles

Set 25 Sheet B, p79

truthful truthfully
untrue untruthful untruly untruthfulness untruth

Set 26 Sheet B, p82

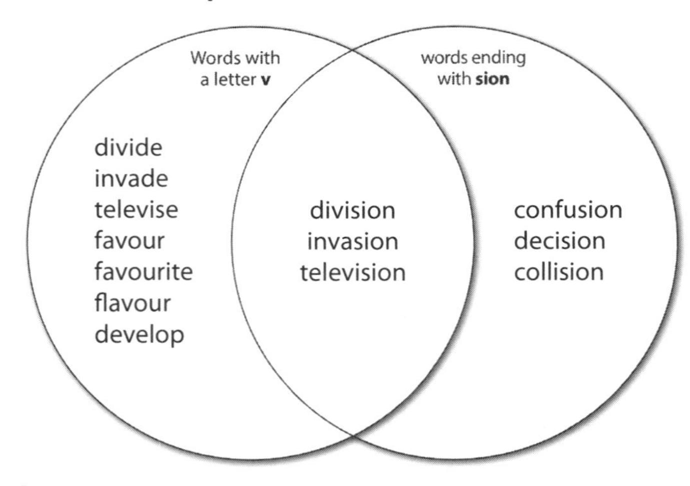

confuse decide collide

Set 27 Sheet B, p85

our: humour vigour flavour favour glamour
ous: curious humorous vigorous outrageous hideous serious spontaneous glamorous courageous obvious courteous
age: outrage courage

Possible extra words ending in age: advantage anchorage average baggage carriage

Set 28 Sheet B, p88

and: expand
end: tend intend extend attend pretend
sion: extension expansion tension comprehension
tion: attention intention
sive: comprehensive extensive expansive

Possible extra words:
and: stand understand hand band land island
end: friend commend comprehend defend lend mend spend recommend
sion: decision discussion television permission admission confusion
tion: abbreviation objection dejection collaboration infection proportion
sive: adhesive exclusive sensitive expensive impressive persuasive

Set 29 Sheet B, p91

logic: logical logically illogical logician
medicine: medical medicate medication medically
tradition: traditional traditionally traditionary untraditional
chemistry: chemist chemical chemically
season: seasonal unseasonal seasonable seasonably

Answers

Set 30 Sheet B, p94

1. microscope, microbe 2. microphone 3. minibeasts
4. minibus 5. minimum 6. miniature

small: tiny mini miniature minute little petite puny teeny etc.
large: big giant gigantic huge enormous massive grand immense colossal etc.

Set 31 Sheet B, p97

science/scientific chemistry scientist choir scene chorus character

scheme chemist discipline chemical fascinate choral echo scientific crescent

Set 32 Sheet B, p100

Sentence to include baby's
Sentence to include babies'
Sentence to include girl's
Sentence to include girls'
Sentence to include boy's
Sentence to include boys'

Set 33 Sheet B, p103

actual bicycle calendar disappear extreme grammar increase mention notice position probably straight therefore various whose woman

actual actually
extreme extremely
various variously
straight straightly

Set 34 Sheet B, p106

accident breath caught century describe eight famous group height important knowledge library minute occasion ordinary perhaps

famous famously
accident accidentally
occasion occasionally
important importantly
ordinary ordinarily
minute minutely

Set 35 Sheet B, p109

actually breathe centre different exercise fruit heart island naughty particular promise remember strength through weather weigh

naughty naughtily
particular particularly
different differently

Set 36 Sheet B, p112

accidentally although believe circle earth favourite guard imagine medicine occasionally potatoes quarter reign separate surprise who's

medicine: medical medicate medication medically
favourite: favour favouring favoured favourable favourably favouritism unfavourable unfavourably
imagine: imagining imagination imagined unimagined imaginable unimaginable
surprise: surprised surprising unsurprising surprisingly unsurprisingly

Set 37 Sheet B, p115

address build certain decide experience February guide history learn natural pressure question recent sentence though whether

January 31	May 31	September 30
February 28 or 29	June 30	October 31
March 31	July 31	November 30
April 30	August 31	December 31

Set 38 Sheet B, p118

answer busy complete consider difficult early forward heard length material often popular possess special suppose weight

possess: possession possessed possessing
consider: considered considering consideration considerable considerably inconsiderable

Set 39 Sheet B, p121

appear business continue eighth enough experiment forwards interest opposite peculiar possession purpose regular strange thought women

appear: appeared appearing appearance disappear disappeared disappearance
thought: thoughtful thoughtfully thoughtfulness thoughtless thoughtlessly thoughtlessness

Set 40 Sheet B, p124

knighthood friendship neighbourhood relationship
championship livelihood childhood ownership partnership

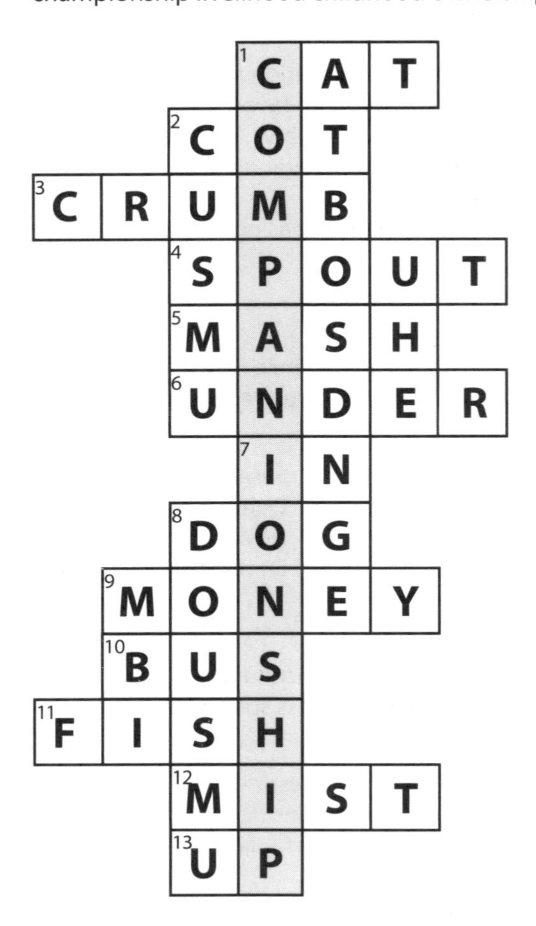

Puzzle word: companionship

Summary

You may wish to photocopy this page and cut it into sets, so that you can give your children a list of the words they will be focusing on each week.

Set 1

shoot
shot
catch
caught
fight
fought
hear
heard
shake
shook
wear
wore
creep
crept
break
broke

Set 2

calf
calves
half
halves
self
selves
cliff
cliffs
sniff
sniffs
knife
knives
life
lives
safe
saves

Set 3

station
ration
competition
question
action
reaction
information
subtraction
serious
ferocious
obvious
previous
curious
glorious
delicious
suspicious

Set 4

ways
always
arm
alarm
so
also
most
almost
one
alone
ready
already
together
altogether
though
although

Set 5

verb
adverb
apt
adapt
venture
adventure
join
adjoin
admit
adjust
advert
addition
admire
adopt
address
advance

Set 6

assemble
assembly
assist
assistant
assort
assortment
attract
attractive
attend
attendance
affix
affirm
afflict
affliction
affection
affectionate

Set 7

bright
flight
alone
aloft
attract
admire
again
ascend
avenue
special
station
enough
subtraction
correction
through
suspicious

Set 8

it's
its
active
captive
forgive
motive
native
massive
expensive
relative
competitive
inquisitive
expansive
corrosive
decisive
attractive

Summary

You may wish to photocopy this page and cut it into sets, so that you can give your children a list of the words they will be focusing on each week.

Set 9

trouble
found
around
journey
route
pour
four
young
taught
caught
aunt
autumn
haunt
cause
because
sausage

Set 10

mission
impossible
missile
hassle
passion
passive
lesson
session
pass
fuss
process
guess
kiss
impress
boss
hiss

Set 11

sadness
kindness
silliness
happiness
drowsiness
darkness
softness
hardness
agreement
appointment
merriment
enjoyment
entertainment
engagement
government
endearment

Set 12

to
too
two
there
their
they're
night
knight
pair
pear
eight
ate
stare
stair
see
sea

Set 13

flat
flatten
sweet
sweeten
tough
toughen
weak
weaken
awake
awaken
alien
alienate
elastic
elasticated
medicine
medicate

Set 14

special
specialise
theory
theorise
personal
personalise
apology
apologise
real
realise
note
notify
jolly
jollify
pure
purify

Set 15

outside
sometimes
without
birthday
something
someone
somewhere
somehow
cupboard
blackboard
fireplace
footwear
anything
everybody
beforehand
another

Set 16

sudden
suddenly
second
secondly
hope
hoping
hopeful
hopefully
decorate
decorative
decoration
wonderful
wonderfully
beauty
beautiful
beautifully

Summary

You may wish to photocopy this page and cut it into sets, so that you can give your children a list of the words they will be focusing on each week.

Set 17

possible
impossible
reversible
terrible
horrible
edible
responsible
indestructible
passable
impassable
laughable
enjoyable
valuable
breakable
agreeable
miserable

Set 18

myth
gym
Egypt
Egyptian
pyramid
mystery
mysteries
gymnast
gymnastics
gymnasium
mysterious
rhyme
rhythm
rhythmic
rhythmical
mythical

Set 19

active
inactive
correct
incorrect
incorrectly
destruct
destructible
indestructible
competent
incompetent
legal
illegal
legible
illegible
logical
illogical

Set 20

regular
irregular
relevant
irrelevant
removable
irremovable
responsible
irresponsible
septic
antiseptic
clockwise
anticlockwise
social
antisocial
climax
anticlimax

Set 21

act
interact
city
intercity
national
international
related
interrelated
heading
subheading
merge
submerge
marine
submarine
network
internet

Set 22

graph
autograph
pilot
autopilot
mobile
automobile
immobile
mobility
biography
autobiography
focus
autofocus
automate
automatic
automation
automatically

Set 23

arrive
arriving
arrived
arrival
occasion
occasional
occasionally
advent
invent
invention
prevent
prevention
interact
interfere
intervene
interrupt

Set 24

humble
humbly
noble
nobly
regular
regularly
basic
basically
frantic
frantically
dramatic
dramatically
music
musically
magic
magically

Summary

You may wish to photocopy this page and cut it into sets, so that you can give your children a list of the words they will be focusing on each week.

Set 25

true
truly
truth
truthful
truthfulness
due
duly
overdue
duration
durable
endure
endurable
unendurable
whole
wholly
wholesome

Set 26

divide
division
invade
invasion
confuse
confusion
decide
decision
collide
collision
televise
television
favour
favourite
flavour
develop

Set 27

humour
humorous
glamour
glamorous
vigour
vigorous
courage
courageous
outrage
outrageous
serious
obvious
curious
hideous
spontaneous
courteous

Set 28

expand
expansion
expansive
extend
extension
extensive
comprehend
comprehension
comprehensive
tend
tension
attend
attention
intend
intention
pretend

Set 29

music
musician
musical
musically
electric
electrician
electrical
magic
magician
magical
magically
politics
politician
mathematics
mathematician
mathematical

Set 30

microscope
microbe
micron
microphone
minibus
minibeast
minicab
miniature
minimum
minimise
little
minor
small
tiny
petite
minute

Set 31

scheme
chorus
choir
choral
chemist
chemistry
chemical
echo
character
science
scientist
scientific
scene
discipline
fascinate
crescent

Set 32

girl's
boy's
baby's
lady's
girls'
boys'
babies'
ladies'
children's
men's
women's
mice's
Cyprus's
James's
Chris's
Jess's

Summary

You may wish to photocopy this page and cut it into sets, so that you can give your children a list of the words they will be focusing on each week.

Set 33

actual
bicycle
calendar
disappear
extreme
grammar
increase
mention
notice
position
probably
straight
therefore
various
whose
woman

Set 34

accident
breath
caught
century
describe
eight
famous
group
height
important
knowledge
library
minute
occasion
ordinary
perhaps

Set 35

actually
breathe
centre
different
exercise
fruit
heart
island
naughty
particular
promise
remember
strength
through
weather
weigh

Set 36

accidentally
believe
circle
earth
favourite
guard
imagine
medicine
occasionally
potatoes
quarter
reign
separate
surprise
although
who's

Set 37

address
build
certain
decide
experience
February
guide
history
learn
natural
pressure
question
recent
sentence
though
whether

Set 38

answer
busy
complete
consider
difficult
early
forward
heard
length
material
often
popular
possess
special
suppose
weight

Set 39

appear
business
continue
eighth
enough
experiment
forwards
interest
opposite
peculiar
possession
purpose
regular
strange
thought
women

Set 40

brotherhood
knighthood
livelihood
neighbourhood
childhood
falsehood
friendship
membership
relationship
hardship
companionship
partnership
workmanship
craftsmanship
companionship
ownership